MULTINATIONAL RESTRUCTURING, INTERNATIONALIZATION AND SMALL ECONOMIES

Much of the existing literature of multinational companies has been concerned with firms originating in the world's largest economies. This book redresses this situation by presenting important information on internationalization of a small country's industry. *Multinational Restructuring, Internationalization and Small Economies* goes beyond traditional studies of foreign direct investment. By using detailed data covering practically all Swedish multinationals and more than two decades of expansion in international markets, the authors describe, interpret and analyse issues which are normally difficult to investigate. These include:

- the predominance of take overs as mode of entry;
- the growth of intra-firm trade;
- the internationalization of technology;
- the effects of European integration and the increase in Swedish FDI and changes in the organization of corporate activity.

The work provides new evidence on the links between foreign production, on the one hand, and trade, development and diffusion of technology, employment and regional integration on the other. Home to many prominent multinationals, Sweden represents a particularly interesting case study.

This book was mainly written at the Industrial Institute for Economic and Social Research (IUI), Stockholm. **Thomas Andersson,** previously in charge of the International Research Programme at IUI, is currently Head of the Structural Policy Secretariat, Ministry of Industry and Commerce, Stockholm. **Torbjörn Fredriksson,** a former research fellow at IUI, is Head of Division, Ministry of Industry and Commerce. **Roger Svensson** is a research fellow at IUI.

ROUTLEDGE STUDIES IN INTERNATIONAL BUSINESS AND THE WORLD ECONOMY

MULTINATIONAL RESTRUCTURING, INTERNATIONALIZATION AND SMALL ECONOMIES

The Swedish Case

Thomas Andersson, Torbjörn Fredriksson, Roger Svensson

Routledge
Taylor & Francis Group

LONDON AND NEW YORK

First published 1996
by Routledge
2 Park Square, Milton Park, Abingdon, Oxon, OX14 4RN

Simultaneously published in the USA and Canada
by Routledge
605 Third Avenue, New York, NY 10017

*Routledge is an imprint of the Taylor & Francis Group, an informa
business*

Typeset in Garamond by Pure Tech India Ltd, Pondicherry

British Library Cataloguing in Publication Data
A catalogue record for this book is available from the British
Library
Library of Congress Cataloging in Publication Data
A catalogue record for this book has been requested

Publisher's Note
The publisher has gone to great lengths to ensure the quality
of this reprint but points out that some imperfections in the
original may be apparent

ISBN 13: 978-0-415-12286-3 (hbk)

ISSN 1359–7930

CONTENTS

FIGURES

vii

TABLES

TABLES

ABOUT THE AUTHORS

This book was mainly written at the Industrial Institute for Economic and Social Research (IUI), Stockholm. Thomas Andersson, previously in charge of the International Research Programme at IUI, is Head of the Structural Policy Secretariat, Ministry of Industry and Commerce, Stockholm. Torbjörn Fredriksson, a former research fellow at IUI, is Head of Division, Ministry of Industry and Commerce. Roger Svensson is a research fellow at IUI.

FOREWORD

This book would not have been possible had it not been for the extensive database at the Industrial Institute for Economic and Social Research (IUI) in Stockholm. This rich resource gathers information provided by generations of executives from most Swedish companies with affiliates abroad. They kindly consented to take the time needed to fill in the detailed questionnaire sent out by IUI every fourth year or so. The authors are grateful to Birgitta Swedenborg for her work collecting and structuring the data over the years. Gunnar Eliasson, the previous director of IUI, also played an important role in supporting the project. Gunnar Fors, IUI, assisted in updating the questionnaire to 1990 and participated in several of the studies underlying this book. Jan-Erik Vahlne, Stockholm School of Economics, and his associate Niklas Arvidsson co-operated with the project team. For insightful comments and suggestions for improvements the authors are also grateful to Ulf Jacobsson, director of IUI, Pontus Braunerhjelm, and Karl-Markus Modén, IUI, and Ari Kokko, Stockholm School of Economics. The authors alone are responsible for any errors and omissions.

1

INTRODUCTION

THE WIDER SCOPE OF
INTERNATIONALIZATION

In recent decades, there has been increasing internationalization of previously national economies. While the most conspicuous change is the massive reshuffling of portfolio investment in financial markets, it may be argued that individual economies are more thoroughly affected by foreign direct investment (FDI), through which multinational companies (MNCs) own and control factors of production in foreign countries. In contrast to portfolio investment, FDI involves not only financial flows but also, in particular, transfers of intangible assets, e.g. in the form of knowledge about production processes, markets, distribution channels and management.

The significance of MNCs does not show up only through FDI, but reveals itself in a number of ways. Foreign affiliates account for sales figures which by far exceed the value of all international trade. At the same time, as much as an estimated 30 per cent of all international trade occurs within MNCs, meaning that the same organization serves as both buyer and seller. The cross-border operations of firms play a particularly important role in the international redistribution of technology. MNCs are estimated to account for some 90 per cent of all technology transfers between countries. Their role in the upgrading and spreading of skills in the work force is difficult to evaluate satisfactorily, but is nonetheless known to be paramount.

Today, the internationalization of firms' operations affects the nature of economic activities in virtually every country, whether rich or poor, large or small. Although there have been many

1

studies of FDI, relatively little systematic work has been concerned with MNC structures. Still, the relationship between FDI and trade, employment, technical progress, etc., crucially hinges on the organization of firms. It has therefore become essential to devote more attention to the interplay between the way MNCs are structured and the performance of economies, including policy implications concerning the shaping of economies over time.

Most work in this area has been concerned with MNCs based in the largest industrialized countries. For a number of reasons, those which originate in small countries deserve more careful study. With the domestic market relatively unimportant, for example, firms' ability to exploit economies of scale is crucially related to the prerequisites for international trade and the internationalization of operations. Furthermore, changes in the relative attractiveness of conditions in a small home country and abroad may exert a particularly strong impact on the organization of MNCs, including that of the parent company. Linkages between specific separate firms may also be especially important in such an economy.

Going beyond the traditional flow data studies, this book describes, interprets and analyses developments associated with the expansion of MNCs based in Sweden, which is one of those countries which has been thoroughly affected by FDI. While the underlying data cover the period from 1965 to 1990, special attention is paid to the late 1980s, which have not been investigated and comprehensively summarized in previous published work. The increase in Swedish FDI during these years as well as changes in the organization of MNCs account for new patterns and consequences in notable respects.

CHANGES IN FDI

Along with the much increased volume of FDI, there have been substantial changes in the direction and composition of flows. Consider the following:

1 In the 1970s, FDI shifted away from natural resource extraction and basic manufacturing towards high value-added production, which is critically dependent on access to modern technology and a skilled labour force. In monetary terms, services – particularly related to finance – have overtaken manu-

facturing as the main playing field for FDI. With regard to effects on employment, knowledge creation and production capacity, however, manufacturing continues to be predominant worldwide.

2 Changes have occurred in the way foreign affiliates are established. Reliance on new ventures, so-called greenfield operations, which used to be the predominant mode of entry into foreign markets, has gradually given way to the takeover, or acquisition, of already existing firms.

3 The geographical destination of FDI has been subject to several large shifts. The United States attracted a sharply increased share of world FDI in the early 1980s, and has remained a prominent recipient since then. The integrating economies in Western Europe became a major target in the late 1980s. Although the booming East Asian region has also received an enhanced share, the developing world as a whole declined in importance during that decade. This trend was reversed in the early 1990s as flows to Asian countries expanded even further and Latin America also received increased FDI.[1] Eastern Europe and parts of Africa were also the object of new interest among investors. Still, the bulk of FDI has so far been directed to the major industrialized countries.

4 Finally, there has been a geographical diversification of the national origin of MNCs. The second and third columns in Table 1 show the distribution in OECD[2] countries of the stock of outward FDI in 1980 and 1990 respectively. The fourth column depicts the change that occurred between these years in each country's weight as a source of investment. The predominant reduction was recorded for the United States, which accounted for almost 44 per cent of the total stock in 1980. By the end of the decade its share had plummeted to 27 per cent. The United Kingdom, which had the second largest stock at the outset, also retreated. The most rapid growth was recorded for Japan, whose internationalization started relatively late. Most of the smaller economies in Western Europe also became more important sources of outward FDI.

The connection between MNCs and nation states has been subject to a major transformation. Gone are the days when foreign investors were simply resented as the carriers of evil. Most governments are now attempting to make their country an attractive

3

Table 1 Outward stock of FDI relative to GDP, 1990, and share of total outward stock of FDI in the OECD, 1980 and 1990, by country, per cent

Countries	GDP US$ billion 1990	Share of outward stock of FDI in the OECD 1980	Share of outward stock of FDI in the OECD 1990	Change in the share of OECD FDI between 1980 and 1990	Outward stock of FDI/GDP in 1990
United States	5,464.8	43.8	26.9	−16.9	7.9
United Kingdom	974.1	16.0	14.3	−1.7	23.5
Germany	1,496.4	8.6	9.5	+0.9	10.1
Netherlands	283.6	8.4	6.8	−1.6	38.2
France	1,192.2	4.7	6.9	+2.2	9.2
Canada	566.7	4.5	4.7	+0.2	13.4
Switzerland	226.0	4.3	4.1	−0.2	29.1
Japan	2,940.4	3.3	12.6	+9.3	6.9
Italy	1,094.8	1.4	3.5	+2.1	5.1
Belgium[a]	201.3	1.2	1.8	+0.6	14.4
Sweden	227.9	1.1	3.1	+2.0	21.9
Australia	293.9	0.4	1.9	+1.5	10.5
Denmark	129.3	0.4	0.5	+0.1	5.6
Spain	491.2	0.2	0.9	+0.7	3.1
Norway	105.7	0.2	0.6	+0.4	9.6
Austria	158.2	0.1	0.3	+0.2	2.7
Finland	137.5	0.1	0.8	+0.7	8.8
New Zealand	44.0	0.1	0.3	+0.2	10.0
Turkey	108.6	0.0	0.0	0.0	0.2
Portugal	59.7	0.0	0.0	0.0	0.8

a Including Luxembourg.
Source: OECD (1993b), UNCTAD (1994)

location for MNCs. With the growing complexity of production processes and sharpened international competition, firms are focusing resources on a limited range of demanding functions and continued internationalization appears a prerequisite for the competitiveness of firms and national economies alike. Liberalization is proceeding in goods as well as factor markets, especially on a regional basis.

As the localization of production, marketing and research activities is optimized across national borders, opportunities arise for enhanced welfare worldwide. At the same time, governments as well as their constituents commonly argue that the need to offer favourable conditions to international investors limits their freedom to pursue economic policies as they once did. Monetary and fiscal policies have already been restricted by the responsiveness of financial markets. The mobility of MNCs gives rise to additional concerns with regard to tax policy, labour market institutions, social security systems and environmental legislation. The attraction of skill-intensive activities appears particularly demanding, not least owing to the importance of mutually beneficial synergetic effects and externalities in knowledge creation. Understanding the consequences and the appropriate policy response from the perspective of individual countries or regions requires a more precise picture of firm organization and the way it is changing in response to a variety of circumstances.

THE HOME COUNTRY STILL MATTERS

During most of the history of FDI, the United States has been the dominant source country. Since data on overseas operations are primarily available in the United States, it is understandable that most work on MNCs has focused on firms originating in that country. It has sometimes been argued that the national origin of MNCs is of little importance, and that such concerns are losing whatever significance they once had as firms become skilful at locating *any* activity where it is most efficiently executed.

Although there are partial exceptions, such as Royal Dutch Shell and ABB, the country of origin generally retains a special role for MNCs. Market share remains largest in the home country and production activities are even more concentrated there. The source of innovation, such as research and development (R&D), tends to be especially reliant on headquarters. MNCs from the United States, the United Kingdom, France and Germany typically conduct about 90 per cent of product development activities in their home country, and Japanese firms an even greater share. MNCs still prefer to appoint home country executives to head foreign subsidiaries, although a certain change has been reported in this respect (UNCTAD, 1994). Strategically important corporate functions, such as R&D and governance, consequently con-

5

tinue to draw heavily on the institutions, experience and talent of the home base.

MNCs develop and transfer assets which are unique to companies but which may still differ systematically depending on the characteristics of home countries, implying that the national origin does matter. The broadening of the geographical source of FDI, along with the prevailing focus on the United States in research on MNCs, makes it important to enlarge the scope of study to encompass MNCs based in other countries as well. The small countries which have become the origin of increased FDI, in absolute as well as relative terms, deserve special attention for several reasons.

First, the importance of internationalization for exploiting economies of scale is inversely related to the size of a country's market. While firms based in large countries may have an advantage in enjoying economies to scale, FDI will play a more decisive role in small countries in enabling firms to cover fixed costs required for product development or marketing, for example.

Second, an appropriate understanding of and policy response to various shocks may require consideration of the productive capacity of a country's industry which is located overseas. The foreign operations of MNCs based in small countries may weigh relatively heavily against the industrial apparatus within the national borders.

Third, large individual MNCs may play a relatively important role in small countries, e.g. in terms of trade, employment or knowledge creation. With the accumulation of skills and other intangible assets embodied in specific firms, their actions cannot be assumed to be counterbalanced by the actions of other firms. Such considerations become even more important in smaller economies, which consequently may be particularly strongly affected by the locational decisions of MNCs.

Fourth, FDI related to small countries is likely to be the most affected by regional market integration. This partly reflects the fact that the relative significance of the national market changes more in a small country when borders are removed. With the liberalization process in Western Europe, for example, there have been major alterations in the pattern of FDI both within and outside the integrating economies in the European Union (EU), previously the European Community (EC). The changes in investment have, in turn, affected the preconditions of the integration process itself.

In fact, three of the four countries which have the largest stock of outward FDI relative to the size of the economy can be said to belong to the category of small countries, given that Great Britain is regarded as medium-sized. Together with this historically leading source country, the Netherlands, Switzerland and Sweden had stocks of outward FDI exceeding 20 per cent of GDP in 1990. These countries have a high dependence on trade, a strong base of skilled labour, high R&D intensity and a history of successful innovation. For large economies such as the United States and Japan, the corresponding shares were 8 per cent and 7 per cent respectively. However, while those countries which can be expected to be the most affected by outward FDI are relatively small, there has been a tendency for inward investment to focus on the industrial core of large economies.

For such reasons, there are a number of research issues which need to be reviewed from the perspective of small countries. Because the very foundation of MNCs is associated with ownership-specific advantages, a great deal of work remains in order to settle the empirical facts. In the case of official statistics, the international operations of firms can generally be only vaguely derived from flow data regarding FDI. What matters is rather information on international operations themselves, including the structures within firms. Detailed data on MNCs' operations in foreign countries is seldom available, and intra-firm data are almost completely lacking.

UNIQUE DATA

This study draws on a database collected since the mid 1960s by the Industrial.Institute for Economic and Social Research (IUI) in Stockholm, and most recently updated to 1990. The data cover virtually the whole population of Swedish MNCs in manufacturing. Containing detailed quantitative information on activities in the source country as well as in host countries, it opens up opportunities for the study of issues which can seldom be analysed on the basis of official statistics. In fact, no other information set covers MNCs from a single country equally well in terms of either scope or detail. Nowhere else are comprehensive time-series data available on the operations and transactions of individual MNCs and affiliates.

Analyses of the IUI data up to 1986 were published by Swedenborg (1979; 1982) and Swedenborg et al. (1988), most of which are available only in Swedish. The trends previously investigated have here been updated as far as possible (see Appendix A). The speed of internationalization, changes in industrial and country characteristics, the frequency of establishments, etc., are reported so as to allow comparability over time. In some cases, results are presented for 'identical companies', i.e. those for which information is available from each questionnaire over a certain time period. This may, for instance, be practised when an important change in the population has been caused by major firms failing to answer specific questions.

The 1990 survey covers Swedish industrial firms with more than 50 employees and with at least one majority-owned foreign affiliate. A total of 329 MNCs responded to the questionnaire, a response rate of 94 per cent. The sample consists of 119 MNCs with and 210 MNCs without manufacturing affiliates abroad. The book focuses on the activities of the former, which have contributed information for the group of companies as a whole as well as for each individual affiliate producing abroad.[3]

Table 2 reports figures for the 119 company groups which have completed the full 1990 IUI questionnaire.[4] Together, these MNCs encompassed 713 majority-owned foreign manufacturing affiliates. Compared with the survey which was conducted in 1986, this corresponds to a net increase of 11 MNCs and 67 subsidiaries. Throughout the book, unless otherwise stated, classifications are made according to the industrial characteristics of the parent company.[5] The population is dominated by the engineering sector, represented by 61 MNCs and 426 foreign affiliates. Within engineering, the metal products industry accounts for the greatest number of companies, while electronics and transport dominate in terms of sales and employment.

More than a quarter of total sales from Swedish MNCs originates in the basic industries of paper/pulp and iron/steel, which have a strong dependence on natural resources and a comparatively low share in employment terms. The 19 chemical MNCs with their 115 foreign affiliates were responsible for about 10 per cent of the population's total sales and employment, whereas their contribution to value added was more than 12 per cent. The group of 'other industries' includes sectors such as food production, textiles and clothing, paper and wood products, cement as well as optical instruments.

Table 2 Swedish multinational companies in manufacturing, by industry of parent, 1990

Industry	Number of MNCs	Number of majority-owned manufacturing foreign affiliates	Percent of Sales	Employees	Value added
Basic industries	12	88	28.0	21.9	26.0
Paper and pulp	7	66	21.4	17.2	20.5
Iron and steel	5	22	6.6	4.7	5.5
Chemicals	19	115	10.6	9.4	12.2
Engineering	61	426	54.0	62.7	55.5
Metal products	27	118	5.5	6.5	7.1
Machinery	19	126	11.4	14.5	13.6
Electronics	11	162	19.9	28.5	22.2
Transport	4	20	17.2	13.3	12.5
Other industries	27	84	7.4	6.0	6.3
Food and drink	4	5	1.3	0.6	0..6
Textiles and clothing	6	8	0.3	0.3	0.3
Paper products	6	24	2.9	2.9	2.6
Miscellaneous	11	47	2.9	2.2	2.8
All industries	119	713	100	100	100
Total	119	713	663,888 (SEK million)	777,710	236,964 (SEK million)

Note: Paper and pulp – ISIC 341, Iron and steel – ISIC 37, Chemicals – ISIC 35, Metal products – ISIC 381, Machinery – ISIC 382, Electrical machinery and electronics – ISIC 383 (denoted electronics), Transport equipment – ISIC 384 (denoted transport), Food and drink – ISIC 31, Textiles and clothing – ISIC 32, Paper products – ISIC 342, Miscellaneous – ISIC 33, 36, 385 and 39.
Source: IUI database

Although firms with fewer than 50 employees, foreign-owned firms in Sweden or sectors other than manufacturing are not covered by the IUI survey, a comparison with official data shows that the MNCs included correspond to at least 91 per cent of total foreign employment in Swedish manufacturing firms, and about 83 per cent when all sectors are included. Furthermore, the SEK 33 billion reported in the IUI data as the initial value of fixed assets in all foreign enterprises acquired in 1990 by Swedish MNCs can be compared with the SEK 35 billion of outward FDI in manufacturing as reported by the Swedish central bank for that year.[6] Although statistics from the two sources are far from fully compatible, as the FDI statistics concern only cross-border financial flows, this further attests to the broad coverage of FDI by the firms in the IUI survey.

It may be noted that manufacturing has accounted for a declining share of Swedish FDI. From the early 1970s, when this sector was responsible for 90 per cent of the total, it fell to 62 per cent on average in the period 1983–6 and 49 per cent in 1987–90. The relative decline of manufacturing is likely to be overestimated, however, since these figures do not encompass reinvested earnings. According to central bank statistics, reinvested earnings amounted to SEK 51 billion in the period 1987–90, corresponding to almost 30 per cent of the total outward flow of FDI.

CONTENT OF THE BOOK

As the IUI data have been updated to 1990, it is now possible for the first time to investigate the characteristics and consequences of the great expansion of FDI from Sweden which occurred in the late 1980s. Regarding the early 1990s, various factors have led to decreased outflows, meaning that the expansion abroad by Swedish MNCs peaked in 1990.

The massive outflows and the modest size of the economy have made Sweden one of the most internationalized countries in the world. With a strong emphasis on manufacturing in FDI, Swedish industry as of 1990 may have had a larger share of operations located abroad than the industrial sector of practically any other country. Analysing trends and events in Swedish-based MNCs up to and including 1990 consequently means tracking causes and effects associated with one of the most dramatic internationalization processes ever seen with regard to outward FDI. During the same period, Sweden received a modest amount of inward investment.

In addition to highlighting developments in Swedish manufacturing MNCs, the content of the book should be of more general interest. Modes of establishment and links between foreign production and trade, technology, training or regional trade liberalization may to a great extent be unrelated to the properties of home countries. Above all, many findings will be of relevance to ventures originating in other small industrialized economies.

Accordingly, international comparisons are presented when similar information is available from other sources. At the same time, it should be stressed that each economy has its own specific conditions. In some countries the service sector entirely dominates FDI, which gives rise to a rather different picture. Thus generalizations to other settings should be made with care. While this always holds true, it is particularly relevant here, owing to the prominent position of idiosyncratic assets in MNCs, as well as the intimate relationship that prevails between the organization of a firm and those specific conditions which it is adapting to. It may be said that FDI represents a process of adjustment to technological, organizational and social change. Its causes and consequences cannot be understood without consideration of the specific set-up it is operating in.

The book is organized as follows. Chapter 2 presents theoretical perceptions of FDI as well as some useful classifications, discusses locational factors and reviews changes that have occurred in the global investment pattern. The background to the development of the Swedish economy, and the internationalization of its industry and MNCs, is sketched in Chapter 3. Furthermore, the forces motivating an increased emphasis on acquisitions rather than greenfield operations as the mode of entry in foreign markets are examined. The relationship between FDI and trade is studied in Chapter 4, with the emphasis on intra-firm trade between parent companies and foreign subsidiaries as well as on the growing importance of the latter as exporters. Results presented in the chapter challenge a number of commonly accepted views regarding the impact of MNCs on trade.

Chapter 5 studies the creation and diffusion of technology, including the organization of R&D, knowledge transfers within MNCs and effects on productivity. Attention is also paid to the linkage between R&D and investment in labour skill. Many of the dramatic changes occurring over time are returned to in Chapter 6, which surveys the connections between corporate internationalization and regional trade liberalization in the European context. Special attention is paid to the restructuring of Swedish MNCs which was triggered by the changed business environment in Europe. Finally, the implications for production structures and social welfare in Sweden are discussed. Chapter 7 sums up.

2

MULTINATIONAL COMPANIES AND NATION STATES

BASIC THEORIES

Along with households, firms are the main actors in the market place, and economic analysis has generally treated them as atomistic and anonymous. Of course, it has long been acknowledged that individual firms, owing to transaction costs and other market imperfections, may grow large and complex with the exploitation of economies of scale and scope. Still, economics has generally continued to judge them on the basis of their external market behaviour.

This approach has been fundamentally challenged by the rise of the MNC, which gains control of equity in foreign markets primarily through FDI. In recent decades, FDI has expanded more rapidly than world income or the total trade in goods. While income and trade almost doubled in value, the stock of FDI quadrupled to an amount corresponding to some 8 per cent of world income (Jungnickel, 1993). Meanwhile, the number of MNCs in the world has increased from 7,000 in the late 1960s to some 37,000 in the early 1990s. It is estimated that these firms control 200,000 affiliates, not counting non-equity links, and that the total sales of foreign affiliates exceed the value of all international trade by some 40 per cent (UNCTAD, 1994).

FDI originally targeted developing countries, and was viewed as a supplement to portfolio investment and inter-industry trade between economies which are inherently dissimilar in terms of comparative advantage. Accordingly, FDI used to be perceived as motivated by differences between countries in the marginal return to capital, in the same way as portfolio investment. The result was a set of macro-oriented theories, based on international trade, e.g.

the currency premium theory (Aliber, 1970), the dynamic comparative advantage theory (Kojima, 1973), and the level-of-development theory (Dunning, 1981).

A set of micro-oriented theories, which instead relate to industrial organization, has gradually become more instrumental for the study of FDI. The product life-cycle theory (Vernon, 1966, 1979) is an early contribution in this field. Noting that firms develop new goods in the industrialized core markets, meaning the United States at the time, but that manufacturing is moved abroad as the output matures and production processes become standardized, Vernon highlighted the influence of product and process characteristics on decisions regarding location.

The main cornerstone of the micro-oriented approach to FDI is the work of Hymer (1960), however. Establishing operations in a foreign environment requires fixed costs, e.g. in obtaining and processing information about local conditions, which become sunk in the host country. On this basis, Hymer concluded that FDI is incompatible with perfect competition, and requires oligopolistic, firm-specific assets. Kindleberger (1969) and Caves (1971) narrowed the gap to neoclassical economics by pinning down factors which may give rise to MNCs: imperfections in goods and factor markets, economies of scale, and government-imposed disruptions. Building on Coase (1937) and Williamson (1975), Buckley and Casson (1976) explained the control of foreign firms by the existence of intangible assets which are difficult to capitalize on in the open market owing to, e.g., imperfections in information, thus favouring the internalization of transactions.

There is a need for both macro- and micro-oriented theories on FDI, depending on what aspects are studied. An analysis of the driving forces or consequences of foreign business operations, however, requires particular attention to the determinants of firm behaviour. Thus the microeconomic theories currently dominate the field. The greatest impact has been exerted by the eclectic approach (Dunning, 1977), or OLI framework, which synthesized much of the earlier theories. According to Dunning, the undertaking of direct investment requires three main pillars: Ownership advantages, Locational advantages and gains from the Internalization of activities within a firm. Examples of firm-specific assets are unique input goods or knowledge emanating from research and development, training expenditures or learning-by-doing.

Internalization may be motivated by difficulties in managing control and governance at arm's length in the presence of diverse information flows.[1] Locational factors may take the form of market size, market growth, factor costs, the availability of infrastructure or suppliers, etc.

Strictly speaking, the OLI framework is not a theory which generates well specified hypotheses for empirical testing. Rather, it forms a conceptual model for how to perceive FDI, and presents a taxonomy of factors which may influence its characteristics. Because ownership advantages are specific to the investing firm, it is difficult to generalize the forces that motivate the internalization transactions, locational determinants and the consequences of investment. In addition, the factors shaping investment decisions continuously change over time. The interplay between technological and organizational forces is shifting the costs and benefits of trading between separate firms relative to internalizing transactions, while economic and social change in transforming the conditions for operating in different countries. Thus FDI is shaped by a mixture of factors on multiple levels.

ORGANIZATIONAL FORMS, OWNERSHIP AND MODES OF ENTRY

In spite of the extensive attention paid to FDI, there is still scanty knowledge of what determines the characteristics of firms' internationalization. Most empirical attempts to explain intra-firm transactions have started out from theories of vertical integration (cf. Williamson, 1971, 1979; Lall, 1978). Hence, internalization has traditionally been seen as an instrument for reducing uncertainty and minimizing the costs associated with the cross-border exchange of goods. Partly depending on the nature of transaction costs, however, international business activities may be organized in various ways. In a crude sense, ventures in manufacturing are integrated in MNCs either vertically or horizontally (Caves, 1971, 1982).

Vertical integration means locating separate stages of the value-added chain in different countries while retaining common control. The category was initially seen as comprising either forward or backward integration with regard to the parent company. Nowadays, corporate structures have become highly complex, with vertical linkages running back and forth.[2] Each activity is, in principle, located where it is most efficient, indicating an advanced form of international intra-firm specialization of the value-added chain. Affiliated units complement rather than replicate each other. The costs of co-ordinating and transporting intermediate goods are outweighed by efficiency gains from concentrating and specializing production in certain locations. In that case, operations are adapted to the specific conditions of the host country, yet closely integrated with operations elsewhere. Trade liberalization, dissimilar technologies in different stages of production, variation in factor prices and economies of scale at the plant level favour this kind of organization (Casson and associates, 1986).

In contrast, horizontal integration implies that operations resemble those organized by the MNC in other places, but without intense interaction between plants, at least as far as intermediate products are concerned. Each affiliate produces for a certain market while the competitiveness of the group of companies emanates from, e.g., a patent or a brand name. Production tends to be standardized but, owing to high costs of transport or exchange of information, benefits from proximity to customers. In that case, country differences in factor costs or economies of scale at the plant level are not sufficient to motivate international specialization of operations.

The two models of organization are neither mutually exclusive nor exhaustive, seldom appear in their pure form and overlap within MNCs as well as within affiliates. There are other models, such as conglomerate expansion, which implies the manufacturing of a diversified product line with few connections between the constituents. A common motive for this organizational form has been the spreading of risk, e.g. by mixing activities which are differentially sensitive to changes in the business cycle. However, this kind of structure has generally become less prevalent as firms have felt under pressure to concentrate resources on core lines of business (Wernerfelt and Montgomery, 1988; Porter, 1991). In contrast, strategic motives, which aim at raising the competitiveness of an MNC as a whole by countering the moves of competitors, have become more important in shaping investment decisions. On the basis of scope with regard to products, markets and value added, one approach (White and Poynter, 1984) has classified affiliates into: the marketing satellite business, the miniature replica, the rationalized manufacturer, the product specialist and the strategic independent. Of these, the rationalized manufacturer and the product specialist tend to have most vertical links, the miniature replica has obvious traits of horizontal integration, while the strategic independent is common in conglomerates. As individual affiliates will not be classified here, it will be sufficient for the purposes of the present study to reason in terms of the two major forms of integration.

So far, it has been assumed that ownership ensures efficient control and governance, making it possible to overcome agency problems such as those associated with moral hazard and adverse selection. Yet the extent to which internalization represents a solution cannot be taken for granted. Grossman and Hart (1986) take the position that internalization does not affect such problems at all. In practice, the costs and benefits of internalization will be influenced by the nature of operations, including the characteristics both of the parent company and of affiliates.

Establishing majority-owned affiliates is just one way in which firms internationalize operations. Joint ventures, management contracts, licensing agreements, alliances between separate firms operating at arm's length, etc., represent a range of alternative approaches which involve a varying degree of foreign control and commitment. The rational for tight control increases with the presence of transaction costs, which are likely to be particularly high in activities subject to heavy dependence on modern technology and human skill. At the same time, control tends to be more costly and risky the less information a company has about local conditions. For such reasons, smaller companies, which have less ability to cover large fixed costs, may prefer a strategy which involves less control and more risk-sharing (Caves, 1982).

While many firms originally start out with an agent, licensing or some loose form of partnership with a domestic firm, more or less fully owned foreign affiliates usually attain a key role in the internationalization of the mature MNC. Broadly speaking, a foreign affiliate is established either as a new venture, i.e. through greenfield operations, or by the acquisition of an existing company. According to Caves (1982), the choice can be interpreted as a trade-off, with new ventures being more risky than take-overs but rendering a higher expected rate of return. More fundamentally, the two modes of entry raise different issues with regard to control. A new venture can be tailor-made to fit the existing MNC network of assets and relations. Acquisition means taking advantage of already established assets but having to adapt them to the interests of the parent company.

As will be seen in the following chapters, new ventures are generally more inclined to import intermediate products from the home country than acquired affiliates.[3] This indicates relatively large 'embodied' technology transfers from parent companies to new ventures. Acquired affiliates, which are now predominant, are marked by their own corporate culture and connections with local subcontractors and suppliers. In that case, knowledge transfers may well be running in either direction (Cantwell, 1989; Kogut and Chang, 1991). Undertaking acquisitions with the purpose of securing access to know-how may be referred to as 'technology sourcing'.

LOCATIONAL DETERMINANTS OF FDI

As long as the United Kingdom and the United States were the main sources of FDI, it seemed natural to ask why firms from these countries chose to establish operations abroad. The significance of this perspective was made explicit in the work of Vernon (1966, 1979). As in the traditional macroeconomic theories on MNCs, it has generally been argued that FDI expands with differences between countries in production costs. This remains a major characteristic of many newer locational theories (Markusen, 1984; Helpman and Krugman, 1985; Ethier and Horn, 1990).

Considerations of this sort are mainly relevant in the case of vertically organized MNCs. Portfolio diversification (Grubel, 1968), which is most applicable to conglomerate expansion, similarly motivates flows between inherently different economies. However, a number of studies have found that labour cost differentials do not play a major role in explaining location decisions (Scaperlanda and Mauer, 1969; Swedenborg, 1979). In fact, the geographical patterns which are predominant require other explanations. The bulk of FDI consists of flows between developed countries within the triad of industrialized countries in North America, Western Europe and East Asia.

The prevailing investment patterns have been interpreted in different ways. As noted above, UNCTAD (1993) largely associates the expansion of FDI in the triad with a deepened international specialization of production, meaning a more complex interaction between vertically integrated units. Markusen (1994) rather views

17

FDI between developed countries as an indication of horizontal integration. In practice, the forces determining localization will vary depending on MNCs' organization, which shows up in marked differences between industries as well as between individual MNCs.

For either kind of investment, location decisions are strongly dependent on the specific historical and geographical context. The establishment-chain theory (Johanson and Vahlne, 1977; Cauvisqil, 1980) highlighted the role played by the need to reduce risk and uncertainty. According to this framework, foreign affiliates are established where trade has previously been intensive, and market penetration as well as learning have already advanced to a high degree. Indeed, most ventures are initially located in neighbouring countries, whence MNCs gradually expand to more distant markets. Tsurumi (1976) discussed the initial targeting by Japanese FDI of South East Asia. French MNCs first located foreign production activities in adjacent European countries and in their ex-colonies (Michalet and Delapierre, 1976). Swedish firms began their internationalization in other Scandinavian countries before establishing operations in the rest of Europe, North America, Latin America, and so forth (Swedenborg, 1979; Johanson and Vahlne, 1977).

Barriers to trade and investment also play an important role in determining FDI. Analysing the choice between overseas production and exports, and taking monopolistic competition into consideration, the proximity concentration theory holds that FDI is motivated by advantages of proximity to customers or specialized suppliers as determined by various barriers rather than economies of scale at the plant level relative to the corporate level (Krugman, 1983; Horstman and Markusen, 1992; Brainard, 1992). This is empirically supported by Brainard (1994) in the case of United States MNCs.

It should be noted that various ventures must not be analysed in isolation. Owing to its possession of firm-specific assets, one MNC will not automatically be replaced by another. Thus certain organizations and functions may be interdependent, creating benefits from co-location (Schumpeter, 1939). A situation of many firms making simultaneous location decisions, each influenced by others, may be subject to 'strategic complementarities' (Cooper and John, 1988). The 'optimal' amount of investment in a country by one firm increases with the undertaking of investment by others, especially in innovative activities. This makes it important to consider 'systems' rather than bipolar relations.

Several studies have found evidence of spatial concentration, or agglomeration effects, in the location of FDI. Knickerbocker (1973) and Vernon (1983) noted that markets may be entered by groups of competing firms, i.e. either 'none' or 'all' rivals enter. In a study of FDI by the United States, Wheeler and Mody (1992) found agglomeration economies to be the major locational determinant. In the developing world infrastructure quality played a central role, while 'specialized support services', such as those related to previous investment, were crucial in industrialized countries. This points to a self-enforcing process in which FDI accounts for additional FDI. Further evidence of agglomeration is found in the pattern of Japanese ventures in Europe, which has been argued to strengthen the prevalent specialization of countries and regions but also to create new patterns (Micossi and Viesti, 1991; Andersson, 1993a).

The literature on locational factors has primarily focused on conditions in host countries. In practice, it is clear that FDI is affected not only by 'pull' factors, but also by 'push' factors which are associated with the home country, or with the relations between the home base and foreign markets. Such considerations are likely to be particularly important to MNCs whose production apparatus is unrelated to country-specific factors, and whose home market is of relatively small importance.

In the presence of barriers to trade, it has been argued, large economies will foster relatively large companies and small countries will specialize in production based on no returns to scale (Krugman, 1980; Venables, 1987). On the other hand, a small domestic market provides firms with a stronger incentive to achieve economies of scale by exporting and establishing production abroad. In fact, we have already seen that those countries which have the relatively largest outflows of FDI are relatively small, although they represent only a few of all small countries.

In a country whose domestic market is too small for any extensive economies of scale, firms will need to exploit other advantages if they are to grow, with special challenges for innovatory activities. These, in turn, are commonly dependent on synergetic effects in knowledge creation between separate firms, or between firms and universities or research institutes. At the same time, a small economy is likely to have a limited number of potential business partners in a certain activity. This, together with the lesser weight of the domestic market, may suggest that the localization decisions of MNCs based in such a country are particularly sensitive to changes in trade relations, factor prices and other conditions which determine the relative attractiveness of alternative locations for operations.

Summing up, the bulk of FDI occurs between advanced economies. In theoretical as well as empirical work, the prevailing investment patterns are interpreted in terms of either vertical or horizontal integration. In practice, the way MNCs organize their operations will influence the role of both pull and push factors. While firms based in large countries may benefit from economies of scale in the domestic market, small countries may foster MNCs which are particularly mobile internationally. The behaviour of firms may be interdependent because of externalities and agglomeration effects, leading to easy triggering of extensive impacts on investment patterns and, in turn, the conditions prevailing in various countries.

EFFECTS ON NATIONAL ECONOMIES

Through internationalization, firms are able to raise production efficiency, improve access to each market and become more exposed to new knowledge and information. The prospects of firms to a major extent depend on how well they are able to take advantage of such opportunities. From the perspective of countries, however, FDI has often been controversial.

In the developing world, MNCs used to be viewed as an extension of colonialism. This led to many expropriations of foreign assets, especially in resource extraction, with little or no compensation paid. In the late 1970s, however, the developing world shifted to a state in which investors' rights became almost universally respected. One reason is that MNCs reorganized their operations in a way which made affiliates more dependent on the group of companies as a whole. Furthermore, with the expansion of the Eurodollar markets, access to portfolio investment encouraged developing countries to secure a sound reputation as business partners in order to become eligible for borrowing. Above all, countries generally came to view FDI as a package of costs and benefits that they could exploit to their own advantage. Outright competition has evolved between countries for the attraction of

FDI, and not only in the developing world. Most governments have now developed ambitious investment promotion schemes (Kobrin, 1984; Guisinger, 1985; Minor, 1987; Andersson, 1991; Oxelheim, 1993).

The effects of FDI on national economies remain controversial, however. Because of limitations on access to capital, for example, a number of empirical studies have concluded that domestic investment and foreign investment take the form of substitutes, at least in a short to medium term perspective (Stevens, 1969; Belderbos, 1992). In the case of the United States, Feldstein (1994) maintains that each dollar of outward FDI reduces the domestic capital stock by between $0.20 and $0.40.

As MNCs effectively channel liquidity across national boundaries, FDI may be closely connected with portfolio investment. Especially for a small country, the operations of giant MNCs increase the vulnerability of its external position. Since an investor carries the entrepreneurial risk, it is well known that the expected repatriation of profits from FDI must exceed the interest rate. The balance of payments will also be affected via the current account. In a host country, FDI may on the one hand stimulate exports and/or replace imports. On the other hand, foreign-owned subsidiaries tend to be more dependent on imported input goods than domestic firms. From the perspective of the home country, production abroad may substitute for exports, which has been argued to cause a loss of output. At the same time, FDI typically enables firms to expand their overall market shares, which may spur complementary exports, and a strengthening of the parent company as well. These matters will be further examined in Chapter 4.

The costs and benefits directly incurred on the balance of payments from the activities of MNCs must be weighed against other effects. The crucial advantage motivating FDI is generally not associated with privileged financing. Traditional assumptions about the effects on capital formation in host and home countries are of limited use in practice. The main economic significance of FDI emanates from the international restructuring of technology and human skills in production, management, distribution, and so forth. Worldwide, MNCs are the prime innovators as well as distributors of knowledge in production processes and organization.

The impacts of FDI on human resource management have attracted special attention as almost all countries have recorded

21

persistently high unemployment figures. A greenfield investment may be expected to create more jobs in a host country than an acquisition, although especially new ventures which target the local market may threaten jobs in other, competing companies and a take-over may reinvigorate an ailing industry. In practice, the greatest impacts on employment arise in domestic companies connected with, or in other ways affected by, MNCs. According to estimates by ILO, each job created directly by inward FDI would induce another one indirectly.[4] Such relationships are equally relevant from the home country perspective. In any case, attracting foreign investment has mostly been associated with new opportunities for workers while outward flows have been seen as a source of job losses and downward pressure on wages.

However, the net outcome, for employment and in other respects, will critically depend on macroeconomic and institutional conditions, especially in the long term. When general equilibrium effects are taken into account, FDI is commonly argued to offer gains for all countries. Outward FDI and inward FDI both have a potential for improving the allocation of resources, combining underexploited resources with new assets, raising productivity through the adoption and diffusion of new technology and increasing efficiency owing to intensified competition. This way, the exploitation of comparative advantages can proliferate.

On the other hand, it is indisputable that giant MNCs may command tremendous market power. Most empirical studies have found a positive relationship between FDI and market concentration in host country industries, applying both to industrialized and developing countries.[5] However, FDI appears to respond to a high degree of market concentration rather than being the cause of it. In fact, it is now more or less generally accepted that monopolistic powers are boosted through the barriers against the entry of rivalling firms.

Locking investment within the national borders of a source country, or shutting it out from a host country, consequently means preventing opportunities for structural change. At the same time, it has been noted that barriers to inward FDI may be the factor fostering large domestic companies, especially in small countries, resulting in a greater potential for outward FDI (Graham, 1993). Under such conditions, the presence of close interactions between domestic firms is likely to be a prerequisite for building up the competitive assets which enable firms to expand abroad.

This brings us back to the significance of externalities. As clarified by Caves (1982), nation states tend to gain from FDI owing to the presence of beneficial external effects – MNCs simply cannot appropriate all the gains that emanate from their activities.[6] For instance, domestic actors may benefit from 'spill-overs' due to turnover of trained personnel. It has been observed that MNCs tend to pay more for their employees than domestic firms, especially when skill levels are taken into account, which has been interpreted as evidence of the potential for a 'brain drain' to local firms. In many countries, local firms indeed have a high representation of managers who were originally trained by MNCs (Katz, 1987). Spill-overs may also arise through, e.g., forward and backward linkages associated with supplier or distributor relations, demonstration effects and interaction with government officials, to name some additional factors.

It may be said that positive externalities enter the production function of other firms in the form of intermediate goods which are not fully paid for (Griliches, 1979). Such effects tend to be pronounced in knowledge-enhancing activities, as the upgrading of technology and human skills tends to spread to other actors. As introduced by Schumpeter (1939), technological progress may greatly benefit from intense interactions within geographically concentrated clusters, where skills are enhanced among workers, within the educational system, and in networks of suppliers and distributors.

Furthermore, as already discussed above, externalities may give rise to interdependence in behaviour. In view of this, there may be multiple equilibria in the scope and magnitude of FDI, R&D activities or other functions performed by MNCs in a country, and in the quality of the factors of production which go along with it. Locations which offer the most favourable conditions for knowledge creation will attract such activities, while others may specialize in production with less important economies of scale and scope. An equilibrium may be more or less stable with regard to changing industry or country characteristics. Small shifts in initial conditions may give rise to substantial, irreversible reductions in favourable external effects, inflicting long-term losses on society.

The internationalization of business operations has commonly been argued to reduce the role of the nation state. However, governments must take the prime responsibility for externalities and, by specifying the legislative framework and establishing basic institutions, they exert a major influence on the attractiveness of countries as a location for various activities (Freeman, 1982; Cantwell, 1990). In addition to national authorities, this applies to those which are involved in shaping conditions at the regional or local level. Technological externalities are seldom nationwide, but rather function in a limited spatial area. Hence, even a small country may have multiple networks and clusters with a varying degree of common characteristics.

REORIENTATION OF GLOBAL FDI

Along with the expansion of FDI in recent decades, substantial changes have been noted in its sectoral and geographical patterns. Similar to the shifting focus of international trade in goods, ventures exploiting raw materials and low labour costs in developing countries have become much less common. Instead, there has been an advance of manufacturing, with an emphasis on production with a high added value. Meanwhile, FDI has expanded even more dramatically in services, especially in real estate, finance and insurance.

The importance of FDI in services cannot be estimated solely on the basis of investment figures. Ventures may involve an enormous amount of capital, especially in financial services, but the actual content in terms of physical capital or employment may be relatively meagre. In fact, manufacturing tends to remain a focal activity in international business groups. This is particularly the case with MNCs which originate in several of the smaller European countries, even though there are some notable exceptions in this respect. Services are often of prime importance because of their linkages with other activities, such as manufacturing and trade.

Even within traditional manufacturing operations, employees are increasingly involved in varied lines of work, a great many of which can be classified as services. The choice of hardware may, for example, be determined by associated software, financing and after-sales services, etc. In the case of manufacturing in Sweden, Table 3 reports the proportion of services in the total employment of various industries. As can be seen, there was a consistent increase between 1970 and 1991 in most industries, with one-third of all workers in manufacturing engaged in services by 1991, com-

Table 3 Share of services in total employment, by sub-industries,
in Swedish manufacturing, per cent and percentage change,
1970–91

ISIC code	Industry	Year 1970	Year 1982	Year 1989	Year 1991	Percentage change 1991/1970
31	Food, drink and tobacco	25	26	26	26	4
32	Textiles, clothing and leather	18	19	21	18	0
33	Wood products	16	20	19	20	25
34	Pulp and paper	28	32	32	33	18
35	Chemicals, incl. pharmaceuticals	34	38	39	40	18
36	Minerals, concrete, etc.	23	27	26	26	13
37	Iron and steel	25	26	24	25	0
38	Engineering	30	33	32	37	23
39	Other manufacturing	23	28	29	32	39
3	Total manufacturing	27	30	30	33	22

Source: Statistics Sweden

pared with 27 per cent two decades earlier. In chemicals and engineering the share was as high as 40 per cent and 37 per cent respectively, indicating that firms have found it increasingly worthwhile to internalize a range of service functions.

While FDI was primarily directed towards developing regions during the nineteenth and early twentieth centuries, industrialized countries have subsequently become the main target. Economic hardship in the developing world has accentuated this picture. As can be seen from Table 4, Africa and Latin America received a much reduced share of FDI in the 1980s. Conversely, the developing countries in East Asia became highly attractive for FDI. In the 1990s, this region has continued to grow in importance, and other developing countries have rekindled foreign interest as well. This applies especially to Latin America, but also to parts of South Asia. Normalization of conditions in South Africa may alter prospects even in wider parts of sub-Saharan Africa. Meanwhile, the transformation of previously state-planned economies in Eastern

Table 4 Inward stocks of foreign direct investment, by major host region, 1975–90, per cent

Host region	1975	1985	1990
Developed market economies	75.1	75.0	80.8
United States	11.2	29.0	25.9
Western Europe	40.8	28.9	39.5
Japan	0.6	1.0	1.1
Other	22.5	16.1	14.3
Developing countries	24.9	25.0	19.2
Asia	5.3	7.8	9.9
Africa	6.7	3.5	2.0
Latin America	12.0	12.6	7.3
Other	0.9	1.1	0.0
Total	100.0	100.0	100.0

Source: UNCTC (1988) and UNCTAD (1993)

Europe opens up a new area of interest to investors, since wages are very low and expectations of market growth are beginning to pick up.

Thus the coming years may see FDI move into 'new' regions. So far, however, the bulk has been concentrated on the developed market economies of the Western world. During the past few decades, there have been abrupt turns in the direction of these flows. In the early 1980s, the booming, consumption-oriented economy of the United States was the main destination. In the mid 1980s, when the United States was perceived as weakening and the dollar had depreciated, expectations of market growth shifted towards the integrating economies of the EC, as did FDI. With internal trade barriers being phased out, corporations entered eagerly in order to establish positions before others did.

As in the case of the race towards the United States market in the early 1980s, the focus of FDI on Western Europe at the end of the decade partly represented a move by firms based on the periphery towards the major markets. In absolute terms, the largest market economies remain the main source of FDI, and only a few smaller economies can compete even in relative terms. Still, a number of the latter have experienced conspicuously large outflows. This applies to some of the previous West European 'outsiders', which were located on the edge of the integrating Community. Above all, Sweden experienced a dramatic increase in outward FDI.

3

SWEDEN AND THE INTERNATIONALIZATION PROCESS

FROM HIGH GROWTH TO HARDSHIP

Before considering FDI originating in Sweden, let us briefly review the main characteristics of the economy. Traditionally, Sweden has had a well trained and highly qualified work force, productive innovators and entrepreneurs, efficient authorities and a competitive infrastructure. Thus the country has fostered one of the world's most advanced industrialized economies. Forests, iron ore and hydro power were key natural resources laying the foundations of industrialization. During the present century, Sweden has remained a significant exporter of raw materials and raw material-based products. Engineering products dominate overall exports, led by specialities such as motor vehicles, telecommunications, heavy industrial equipment and machinery. In recent years, strong growth has also been recorded in exports of pharmaceuticals. Labour-intensive products, such as textiles, advanced in the early stages of industrialization but diminished in the 1960s as competition increased in standardized products and Swedish wages became relatively high for low skilled workers.

Swedish industry not only has a high capital intensity but, except for Switzerland, it had a higher R&D intensity than any other country during the 1980s, followed closely by Japan, the United States and Germany (OECD, 1989). In addition, industrial R&D has benefited from interaction with extensive academic research. At the same time, the country's specialization *vis-à-vis* the rest of the world, as reflected in its foreign trade, has not demonstrated any similar reorientation towards reliance on R&D-intensive products. Between 1970 and 1990, Swedish engineering exports lost almost 30 per cent of their world market share, while basic products largely maintained their position (Ministry of Finance, 1993; NUTEK, 1994). Although basic industries have become somewhat more knowledge-intensive, the Swedish case represents an example of an economy with a strong base of advanced technology which is not really reflected in its output. Obviously, the technological base located in Sweden itself supports operations on a much broader geographical scale.

The Swedish industrial sector weakened in the 1970s relative to other OECD countries. The oil crises in 1973–4 and 1978–9, and the subsequent worldwide recessions, dealt the Swedish economy a severe blow. An important factor was the triggering of excessive nominal wage increases. Around the end of the decade, the Swedish krona was successively devalued and export-oriented companies found themselves highly competitive. Despite the upturn of the international business cycle, however, employment grew mainly in the public sector, construction – stimulated by extensive subsidies – and the financial sector. These areas absorbed much of the available labour, including skilled workers, while other industries lost out. Wage increases exceeded productivity growth, the opportunity cost of capital rose as securities became highly attractive and there was mounting inflationary pressure. Throughout the 1980s, unemployment rates remained repressed but inflation surpassed the OECD average. Meanwhile, the overall tax burden was by far the highest in the world, and household savings were negative as taxes encouraged borrowing and spending.

By the late 1980s, Swedish policy makers finally agreed to a major tax reform. Although we are primarily concerned with the restructuring which occurred up to 1990, the course of events in the subsequent years should be noted. The international recession deepened and the European Monetary System came under severe pressure, not least owing to the disparity between the economic situation in the unifying German economy and that in most other member countries. As Swedish households adjusted their portfolios in response to the tax reform as well as the international business cycle, cut loans and raised savings to some 8 per cent of GDP, domestic demand contracted abruptly. Along with several other currencies, the Swedish krona could no longer sustain a 'fixed' exchange rate.

As the bubble created by the speculation economy of the 1980s burst, a severe crisis was triggered in the Swedish economy, with soaring interest rates, falling equity values, numerous bankrupt-

Table 5 Annual change in employment in Swedish firms, by company
size, 1985–90 and 1990–2, in per cent

Company size in number of employees	1985–90	1990–2
1–9	+7.5	−11.6
10–99	+14.9	−11.2
100–499	+17.8	−8.9
over 500	−4.2	−14.5

Source: Statistics Sweden

cies and rising unemployment as some of the most conspicuous
features. The financial system was stunned, and most banks were
either nationalized or kept alive through extensive support by the
state, and public finances sharply deteriorated. Small companies,
which were heavily dependent on the domestic market, paid a
heavy toll and many went out of business. Table 5 shows that in
1990–2 employment, which had previously grown in small and
medium-sized firms, now fell drastically in Swedish firms of all
sizes.

Thus what used to be one of the most prosperous societies in the
world, with perhaps the highest level of welfare and the most equal
income distribution, has gradually run into severe difficulties.
Sweden has experienced a decline in real wages and living standards; GDP *per capita* has shrunk below the OECD average, unemployment is only marginally below the West European average
and the budget deficit relative to GDP is among the largest in the
world.[1] A number of studies have pointed to the significance of
regulations which diminished the competitive pressure in the
economy, and made only some 20–25 per cent subject to international competition in 1990.[2] Underlying this development was a
set of circumstances which made the private sector instead grow
outside the country, a trend which is at the heart of the subject of
this book.

As of the mid 1990s, substantial reform and deregulation have
taken place, labour productivity has increased markedly, inflation
is low and costs are at a competitive level. Conditions appear
favourable for a revival of industry. Swedish MNCs have strongly
increased their investment at home, which in some cases has been
associated with disinvestment abroad, and foreign investment into
Sweden has also picked up considerably. In 1994, inward FDI far
outstripped the outward flow for the first time in three decades.

ONE-SIDED INTERNATIONALIZATION

With less than 9 million inhabitants, the Swedish market is of modest size. Exports and imports exceed 30 per cent of GDP, making the economy highly dependent on cross-border exchange. Although manufacturing dropped below 20 per cent of GDP in the early 1990s, it is still responsible for 75 per cent of export revenues.[3] Table 6 shows that the geographical composition of trade has been heavily dominated by the OECD countries. Throughout, Europe has been the most important destination for Swedish exports, accounting for almost three-quarters, with the EC countries absorbing well over half the total. The share of North America grew between 1978 and 1986, after which the EC attained an increasingly dominant position.

The ties with Western Europe have been strengthened through gradual liberalization and economic integration since World War II. In 1960, Sweden and the other Nordic countries took part in the creation of EFTA, which was a response to the formation of the EC a few years earlier. Trade restrictions within and between the two organizations have been abolished, and Sweden had a free trade agreement with the EC since 1973. In the early 1990s, Sweden successively moved towards membership of the EU, which it finally joined on 1 January 1995.[4]

The internationalization has also progressed through large outflows of FDI, particularly in manufacturing, while there has been much less inward FDI. Figure 1 shows inflows and outflows at fixed prices between 1965 and 1993. With few exceptions, the

Table 6 Swedish exports of goods, by destination, 1970–92, per cent

Region	1970	1974	1978	1986	1990	1992
EC	54	53	51	50	54	56
EFTA	21	21	20	20	19	17
North America	8	7	8	13	10	9
Other OECD countries	4	5	4	4	5	5
Developing countries	13	15	17	12	12	13
Total*	100	100	100	100	100	100

Note: EC and EFTA encompass those countries which belonged to the respective organization in 1990; North America encompasses USA and Canada.
*Columns may not add up to exactly 100 due to rounding off.
Source: Statistics Sweden

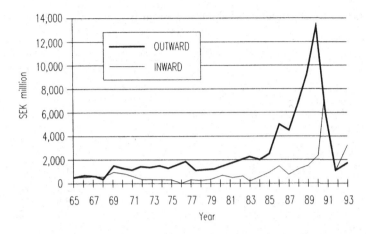

Figure 1 Inward and outward FDI in Sweden, 1965–93, fixed prices
(base year 1968)
Source: Central Bank of Sweden

outflows have exceeded the inflows. The discrepancy was accentuated during the second half of the 1980s when Swedish firms advanced first in the United States, and later in the EC.

Concerning the direction of Swedish outward FDI, Table 7 shows that the EC countries have generally been the main destination. The only exception is the period 1981–6, when the United States attracted increased FDI from everywhere. In the mid 1980s, the European Commission set out the programme for completion of the internal market. The message was reinforced in mid 1987 by the passing of the Single European Act, which constituted a binding commitment to fulfil this goal. FDI in general shifted towards the EC, with Swedish MNCs exceptionally active. Their onslaught peaked in 1990 with a series of large acquisitions. About three-quarters of Sweden's total FDI targeted the EC at that time.

In the mid 1980s, outward FDI increased in relation to gross domestic investment in many OECD countries (see Figure 2). The rise was especially great in a number of small economies in Western Europe, with the single largest increase being that of Sweden. Here, outward FDI rocketed from 6 per cent to 21 per cent of gross domestic investment between the first half of the 1980s and the second. The only countries at a comparable level were the Netherlands and the United Kingdom, which reported much

31

Table 7 Geographical distribution of Swedish outward FDI, 1971–93, per cent[1]

Region	1971–5	1976–80	1981–6	1987–90	1991–3
EC[2]	51.6	42.7	36.8	73.0	64.7
Belgium/ Luxembourg	3.0	3.8	3.4	2.9	− 0.4
Netherlands	6.3	4.3	4.5	16.5	− 5.2
France	6.3	6.5	6.0	1.6	37.4
United Kingdom	9.2	11.5	9.8	20.7	38.4
West Germany	13.7	8.6	4.0	11.7	− 15.2
EFTA[2]	12.3	17.1	11.9	12.0	16.6
United States	11.6	21.5	37.4	9.6	10.5
Other OECD countries	8.0	3.5	2.9	0.4	− 0.2
Non-OECD countries	16.5	15.2	11.0	4.9	8.3
Total	100.0	100.0	100.0	100.0	100.0
Total in SEK millions	8,166	15,427	60,060	175,927	51,974

Notes:
1 Excluding reinvested earnings.
2 The figures for EFTA and the EC cover countries which belonged to the organizations in 1993.
Negative figures means that disinvestment exceeds new investment.
Source: Central Bank of Sweden

larger outflows in previous periods and which were also major recipients of FDI (UN, 1993a).

As discussed in the preceding chapter, it has been argued that large countries are a more important base for the emergence of big companies. Compared with the size of the economy, however, no other country was home to a greater number of the largest 500 corporations on *Fortune*'s list in 1991 than Sweden, which was followed the most closely by Finland and Switzerland (*Fortune*, 27 July 1992; OECD, 1993b). There are a number of reasons for the Swedish position. Industrial innovations in the nineteenth and early twentieth centuries provided the intangible firm-specific assets needed for firms to invest abroad. Beyond this, taxes and labour market institutions, including the role played by the influential trade unions, have favoured large ventures rather than small entities. Weak anti- trust legislation, privileged voting power for certain shares and institutional cross-ownership of equity have

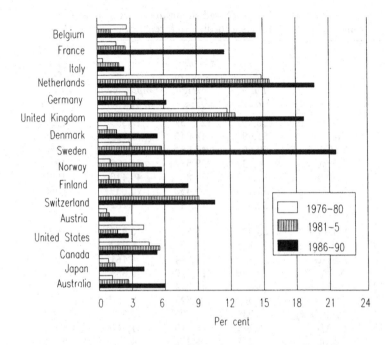

Figure 2 Outward direct investment as a proportion of gross domestic investment, by country (annual average) 1976–80, 1981–5 and 1986–90, in per cent
Source: United Nations (1993)

further led to the establishment of tightly controlled empires, associated particularly with the Wallenberg family. Not only have strategic owners capitalized on the situation, but ironclad structures also been created by management in key organizations, as in the case of Pehr G. Gyllenhammar, Volvo's 'strong man' for more than two decades. Barriers to inward FDI, especially with regard to acquisitions, further strengthened the power of incumbents.

It should also be noted that Sweden has been well endowed with both financial and human capital, the latter partly as a result of early investment in the education system. This, together with government emphasis on the development of an efficient infrastructure, in order to compensate for Sweden's geographical location, has facilitated foreign operations. At the same time, the small size of the domestic market has made it important for companies to expand abroad in order to capture economies of scale. In the

Table 8 The 20 largest Swedish multinational companies in manufacturing, ranked according to foreign employment, 1990

Rank	Company	Total employment	Employment in foreign affiliates	Employment in Sweden	Year of first manufacturing affiliate abroad
1	Electrolux	150,892	123,337	27,555	1921
2	SKF	53,995	48,040	5,955	1908
3	STORA	69,691	47,554	22,137	1956
4	Ericsson	66,138	39,583	26,555	1911
5	Volvo	72,213	22,803	49,410	1958
6	SCA	30,139	19,450	10,689	1960
7	Atlas Copco,	21,507	17,245	4,262	1943
8	Sandvik	26,373	15,850	10,523	1920
9	Alfa-Laval	20,809	15,577	5,232	1885
10	Esselte	19,545	15,084	4,461	1961
11	AGA	14,559	11,870	2,689	1900
12	Nobel	26,654	11,814	14,840	1967
13	Saab-Scania	29,388	8,823	20,565	1957
14	Trelleborg	21,939	8,505	13,434	1960
15	ESAB	8,279	6,319	1,960	1931
16	Euroc	9,207	5,202	4,005	1953
17	Astra	8,846	5,058	3,788	1942
18	Gambro	5,078	4,336	742	1972
19	PLM	6,342	4,306	2,036	1961
20	ASSI	7,633	4,023	3,610	1967
	Total	669,227	434,779	234,448	
	per cent	100	65	35	

Note: With the exception of information regarding year of first foreign establishment, the data presented in the table have been taken from the companies' annual reports. The companies which responded to the IUI questionnaire have been assured that their answers will be kept confidential. In no other table or figure are data reported in a way which makes it possible to identify an individual company.
Source: Annual reports and IUI database

presence of government protection and checks on inward FDI, rivalry between the national champions has been seen as a key factor for generating sufficient competitive pressure (Sölvell *et al.*, 1991).

The modest growth which occurred in the number of Swedish MNCs between 1986 and 1990 was due to some fairly small companies establishing operations in neighbouring European countries for the first time. Most of today's large Swedish MNCs have existed for as long as 70 years. It can be seen from Table 8 that several companies established their first foreign manufacturing affiliate before World War I. Electrolux, which is the top employer in terms of foreign staff, opened its first non-Swedish plant in 1921.[5] All the groups included in Table 8 established their first foreign manufacturing affiliate prior to 1972.

While Sweden has not fostered new large companies during the last 20 years to the extent that it did previously, small and medium-sized companies account for a modest share of the industrial work force by international standards (Braunerhjelm and Carlsson, 1993). Hence, the economy has become heavily dependent on its large MNCs in several respects. The companies included in Table 8 account for more than 30 per cent of total Swedish exports and industrial employment. Their significance is even greater with regard to R&D and innovative capacity.

Many of the factors which shaped and/or preserved the group of large Swedish MNCs have been altered with the upheaval that the economy went through in the early 1990s. Inward FDI has been liberalized and the power structures of the past have been diluted or transformed. Still, the old industrial system will keep influencing the future course of events.

THE INTERNATIONALIZATION OF SWEDISH MNCS

The internationalization of Swedish manufacturing companies accelerated dramatically in the second half of the 1980s from an already high level. Any breakdown of sales, production or employment illustrates that the process advanced to a spectacular degree. Table 9 shows that the share of the home market in the MNCs' total sales declined from 41 per cent in 1970 to less than 23 per cent in 1990. During the same period, the share of total manufacturing output which was provided by the Swedish plants fell from 73 per cent to 46 per cent. Finally, the home country share of the total work force shrank from 64 per cent in 1970 to less than 40 per cent in 1990, with by far the most rapid contraction in the late 1980s.

Over these two decades, considerable expansion has taken place in foreign affiliates. The share of sales affiliates increased from 7

Table 9 Swedish share of Swedish MNC sales, production, value added and employment, 1970–90, per cent

Measure	1970	1974	1978	1986	1990
Sales	41.0	36.3	31.6	27.1	22.6
Production	73.2	70.2	63.2	55.9	46.3
Value added	n.a.	70.7	62.1	55.1	43.5
Employment	64.1	59.8	57.6	50.8	39.8

Source: IUI database

per cent to some 10 per cent. Manufacturing affiliates are of the greatest interest, however, since they generally involve the largest knowledge transfers and affect economic structures the most. In the years between 1978 and 1990, their share of total employment in Swedish MNCs (at home as well as abroad) rose from 31 per cent to 43 per cent. Consequently, the manufacturing units abroad employed a greater number of workers by 1990 than the home operations combined.

As already mentioned, MNCs play a less comprehensive role in employment than they do in, for example, output, trade or R&D. This has become even more the case as MNCs have increasingly expanded their number of employees through the acquisition of existing firms. It can be seen from Table 10, which reports the growth of employment in the manufacturing affiliates of Swedish MNCs in 1979–86 and 1987–90, that a marked trend in this direction has been present both in basic industries and in engineering. Only a modest number of new jobs have been added in greenfield operations, which generally are more important than acquisitions when it comes to generating employment opportunities in the host country. At the same time, a new venture may force domestic competitors out of business, especially if it is targeting the host country's market, while an acquisition may invigorate an ailing industry. Affiliates leaving a group of companies, finally, are generally not closed down, but tend merely to change ownership. All in all, it is difficult to evaluate the impact of FDI on employment in host countries. Again, the most important impacts in this respect are not on job opportunities in affiliates themselves, but arise from linkages with domestic firms. The same applies to the home country as well.

The degree to which Swedish MNCs have internationalized their operations varies a great deal between sectors. Table 11

Table 10 Annual percentage change in number of employees, various categories of manufacturing affiliates of Swedish MNCs, all and selected industries, 1979–86 and 1987–90

Type of industry and affiliate categories	1979–86	1987–90
All industries		
All affiliates	1.6	3.1
Affiliates which have left the group of Swedish MNCs	−6.6	−12.1
New affiliates established through take-over	4.1	9.3
New affiliates established through greenfield investment	2.4	1.5
Basic industries		
All affiliates	3.2	19.4
Affiliates which have left the group of Swedish MNCs	−6.0	− 11.7
New affiliates established through take-over	2.6	21.0
New affiliates established through greenfield investment	2.5	3.1
Engineering		
All affiliates	0.9	3.5
Affiliates which have left the group of Swedish MNCs	−6.7	− 9.5
New affiliates established through take-over	4.0	7.4
New affiliates established through greenfield investment	2.2	1.2

Note: The total number of employees at the beginning of the period serves as a base.
Source: IUI database

Table 11 Distribution of employees in Swedish MNCs, by industry, 1990, number of employees and per cent

Industry	Total employment	Employment in Sweden	Employment abroad	Foreign employment share (per cent)
Basic	170,027	80,692	89,335	52.5
Paper and pulp	133,656	53,452	80,204	60.0
Iron and steel	36,371	27,240	9,131	25.1
Chemicals	72,944	31,852	41,092	56.3
Engineering	487,644	171,542	316,102	64.8
Metal products	50,190	22,446	27,744	55.3
Machinery	113,018	22,169	90,849	80.4
Electronics	221,260	55,984	165,276	74.7
Transport	103,176	70,943	32,233	31.2
Other industries	47,095	22,301	24,794	52.6
All industries	777,710	306,387	471,323	60.6

Source: IUI database

Table 12 Employment in Swedish-owned foreign manufacturing affiliates in developed countries, by industry and region, 1978, 1986 and 1990, number of employees

Industry	EC-6	EC-3	EC-South	EFTA	North America	Other developed countries
1978						
Basic	11,905	5,553	2,647	2,737	4,191	1,753
Chemicals	4,202	1,429	108	2,201	2,076	176
Engineering	62,211	16,700	5,904	6,961	14,976	5,715
Other	14,037	6,527	1,896	3,919	3,697	591
Total	92,355	30,209	10,555	15,818	24,940	8,235
1986						
Basic	7,243	2,824	1,917	1,941	1,505	0
Chemicals	5,313	1,319	223	2,975	4,069	293
Engineering	72,997	18,331	7,637	9,927	39,755	9,621
Other	7,447	5,404	1,659	2,928	8,349	1,252
Total	93,000	27,878	11,436	17,771	53,678	11,166
1990						
Basic	30,023	13,454	2,848	5,189	3,036	21
Chemicals	8,576	2,757	977	2,793	4,625	891
Engineering	72,549	28,237	10,432	6,308	59,460	7,089
Other	3,034	4,546	1,307	1,230	4,045	782
Total	114,182	48,994	15,564	15,520	71,166	8,783

Note: EC-6: Belgium, France, Germany, Italy, Luxembourg and Netherlands; EC-3: Denmark, Ireland and the UK; EC-South: Greece, Portugal and Spain.
Source: IUI database

presents the distribution of employment according to industrial classification of the MNC. In 1990, the foreign share exceeded 50 per cent in most sectors, although there was considerable variation. Transport and iron and steel still retained the bulk of operations in the home country. Machinery and electronics were by far the most internationalized industries, with foreign employment accounting for 80 and 75 per cent respectively of the total work force. As can be seen from the figures, these two industries were the largest in terms of foreign staff but much less important for employment in Sweden.

The distribution of personnel in manufacturing affiliates across regions and industries is shown in Tables 12 and 13 for 1978, 1986 and 1990. In spite of fluctuations, the aggregate trends resemble

Table 13 Employment in Swedish-owned foreign manufacturing affiliates in developing countries, by industry and region, 1978, 1986 and 1990, number of employees

Industry	Africa	East Asia	ASEAN	Rest of Asia	Argentina Brazil Chile	Rest of Latin America
1978						
Basic	30	24	151	1,058	1,554	357
Chemicals	0	0	0	0	2,097	2,187
Engineering	0	0	1,117	2,240	22,739	7,646
Other	126	45	890	382	1,915	479
Total	156	69	2,158	3,680	28,305	10,669
1986						
Basic	0	0	0	0	0	0
Chemicals	0	0	0	0	2,133	2,312
Engineering	34	0	844	4,674	13,615	9,581
Other	457	0	2,109	5,595	3,112	428
Total	491	0	2,953	10,269	18,860	12,321
1990						
Basic	0	0	854	339	0	0
Chemicals	168	0	419	0	2,468	2,864
Engineering	63	262	2,903	4,522	14,528	10,766
Other	242	0	1,701	0	0	0
Total	473	262	5,877	4,861	16,996	13,630

Source: IUI database

those recorded in the global stock of FDI, reported in Table 4. In contrast to world investment patterns, however, Western Europe has been the main location of Swedish FDI all along, especially the EC. After a decline in the first half of the decade, the EC's position revived in the late 1980s. The share of North America increased strongly between 1978 and 1986. In industrialized countries, the total number of employees grew by an annual rate of 2.1 per cent on average in 1979–86, and by 5.5 per cent in 1987–90. In developing countries, by contrast, total employment was stable between 1978 and 1986 and declined by an annual 7 per cent on average from 1986 to 1990.

Regarding industrial patterns, it has been observed for United States and Japanese FDI that R&D-intensive industries have disproportionately small operations in developing countries.

Swedish FDI displays no such picture. Basic industries have predominantly targeted neighbouring European countries, especially leading markets such as Germany. Meanwhile, highly R&D-intensive industries, including chemicals and transport, have a relatively large share of their operations in the developing world.

Regression analysis of the variation in the location of foreign production at the firm level points to the predominance of influences other than those associated with cost levels in host countries. The probability of localization in a country increases with the size of the host country's market, the presence of qualified workers, geographical proximity to Sweden and the extent to which there has previously been close trade relations (Braunerhjelm and Svensson, 1994).[6]

It was further noted in Chapter 2 that MNCs from large home countries tend to concentrate operations in certain locations, possibly owing to knowledge spill-overs. Whether this applies to MNCs originating in small home countries is less clear, not least since useful proxies for agglomeration effects are difficult to construct. The presence of qualified subcontractors, sales networks and other complementary functions, as well as competitors whose moves it may be important to tackle, are likely to be industry-specific in part. An industry's share of total employment in a host country, weighted with the mean of that share in all countries, may consequently serve as one indicator of agglomeration effects. Indeed, this variable was found to exert a significant influence on the locational pattern of Swedish FDI in industries with a high technology content, but with hardly any effect on localization in basic and other industries with lower R&D intensity (Braunerhjelm and Svensson, 1994).

The degree and characteristics of internationalization are also related to the size of firms. While small Swedish MNCs have retained the bulk of their operations at home, the relative importance of the parent company decreases with firm size. Table 14 shows that the largest Swedish MNCs accounted for a growing share of all new affiliates in the 1970s and most of the 1980s. With the European integration process of the late 1980s, however, smaller MNCs became much more active. Compared with 1965–86, MNCs with fewer than 500 employees in Sweden increased their share of new ventures in 1987–90, reaching 27 per cent of the total. The share of firms with more than 10,000 employees declined marginally, from 40 to 37 per cent.

Table 14 Distribution of new foreign affiliates of Swedish MNCs, by parent company size, 1965–90, per cent

Number of employees in parent company	1965–70	1971–4	1975–8	1979–86	1987–90
1–500	11	18	13	14	27
501–1,000	6	9	3	5	9
1,001–5,000	28	19	17	16	16
5,001–10,000	31	22	32	24	11
10,001–	25	32	36	40	37
Total*	100	100	100	100	100

Note: *Columns may not add up to exactly 100 due to rounding off
Source: IUI database

Furthermore, Table 15 shows that the smallest firms have a relatively large proportion of their foreign manufacturing in the neighbouring EFTA countries. These firms do not report any manufacturing in developing countries. The focus on the EC is greatest in medium-sized MNCs, while the largest firms have a sizeable proportion of employment in manufacturing affiliates in developing countries. Note the dominant position in overall employment attained by the 16 MNCs with over 10,000 employees.

Thus, small MNCs have attained a more important role in Swedish outward FDI as far as neighbouring countries are

Table 15 Employment in foreign manufacturing affiliates of Swedish MNCs, 1990, distributed over different regions, by company size, number of employees and per cent

Total number of employees in MNC	Number of MNCs	Number of employees in manufacturing affiliates abroad	Geographical distribution (per cent)				
			EC	EFTA	Other DCs	LDCs	All regions
1–199	28	784	41.0	38.5	20.5	0.0	100.0
200–999	44	6,862	65.5	20.2	10.7	3.6	100.0
1,000–1,999	17	6,763	68.2	6.8	20.4	4.6	100.0
2,000–9,999	14	30,518	68.3	9.8	14.6	7.3	100.0
10,000–	16	270,289	54.9	10.1	19.8	15.2	100.0
Total	119	315,216	57.7	12.7	18.2	11.4	100.0

Source: IUI database

concerned, but large MNCs remain predominant in foreign manufacturing as a whole, especially in distant regions. According to Lindqvist (1991), certain small Swedish firms in high-technology niches have established themselves in non-European markets, but this does not appear as any general tendency in aggregate data. It appears that most small and medium-sized manufacturing firms remain discouraged by the cost of gathering and evaluating information abroad, especially in markets far from the home country.

SHIFT IN OWNERSHIP AND ENTRY MODES

It has already been remarked that the internationalization process has been subject to major changes, not only in terms of geographical and sectoral characteristics but also in respect of organizational forms. A number of studies of Swedish MNCs have indicated the emergence of a 'heterarchical' structure with several formal and informal centres of management and power (Forsgren, 1989, 1990). Individual affiliates were found to have taken on responsibility for a range of functions stretching far beyond the needs of their own markets, although a strong emphasis on the home base appeared to persist in procurement and R&D. The changing structures are partly visible in the ownership of manufacturing affiliates. Table 16a shows that a growing share is one hundred percent-owned by the MNC, either directly or indirectly. Between 1978 and 1990, the share of wholly-owned subsidiaries rose

Table 16(a) Percentage of affiliates directly or indirectly wholly-owned by the parent company of the MNC, by region, selected years 1965–90

Region	1965	1970	1974	1978	1986	1990
EC-6	76	86	78	72	85	88
EC-3	80	92	94	92	91	94
EC-South	46	70	61	64	80	64
EFTA	77	82	85	83	87	85
North America	79	90	92	85	92	92
Other DCs	78	70	85	88	81	74
Africa	67	67	33	50	33	60
Asia	38	36	25	40	25	65
Latin America	78	84	68	70	63	82
All regions	75	83	79	77	83	86

Note: See note to Table 12.
Source: IUI database

Table 16(b) Percentage of affiliates over 50 per cent directly owned by the parent company of the MNC, by region, selected years, 1965–90

Region	1965	1970	1974	1978	1986	1990
EC-6	88	84	75	61	48	32
EC-3	96	93	92	62	48	36
EC-South	100	87	81	82	67	50
EFTA	81	79	90	74	70	66
North America	100	97	89	51	43	36
Other DCs	67	40	50	30	44	44
Africa	100	100	100	100	67	50
Asia	69	79	75	73	63	53
Latin America	90	88	83	70	71	74
All regions	88	84	81	63	54	44

Note: See note to Table 12.
Source: IUI database

from 77 per cent to 86 per cent on average. In less developed countries, including southern EC countries, there is a greater degree of mixed ownership, which is mainly an effect of national regulations.

As can be seen in Table 16(b), however, the direct influence of the parent company has diminished markedly. Almost 90 per cent of all manufacturing affiliates of Swedish MNCs were more than 50 per cent directly owned by the parent company in 1965, which applied to less than half in 1990. Thus, foreign holding companies within the MNCs became much more prominent in ownership. With regard to different regions, North American affiliates are to a very high degree owned directly by affiliated companies other than the parent, whereas the opposite is true in EFTA and Latin America. This reflects the higher turbulence in corporate structures in the former region.

Meanwhile, we have seen that the take-over has generally become more important as entry mode in foreign markets. This is clearly visible in the behaviour of Swedish MNCs. Figure 3 illustrates a systematic shift in the way manufacturing affiliates have been established by Swedish MNCs across regions over time. The share of acquisitions has been higher in industrialized countries than in the developing world, and particularly high in the EC. Still, each region has experienced an equally steady trend towards increased emphasis on acquisitions.

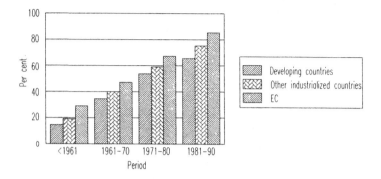

Figure 3 Proportion of acquisitions in different regions over time, per cent
Source: Andersson and Svensson (1994)

At a more disaggregated level, the variation in entry modes reveals interesting irregularities. Table 17 shows that take-overs by Swedish MNCs have remained infrequent in Japan, which is in line with observations of FDI from other countries. The share of take-overs has continued to be low in the rest of Asia as well. In Latin America, on the other hand, the proportion of take-overs grew to some three-quarters of the total in the 1980s, which was about the same level as in the EFTA countries.

With growing international experience, it might have been expected that firms would become increasingly capable of mastering the risks involved in greenfield operations. This conflicts with the reverse trend in entry modes observed in most regions. Zejan (1990) argued that the actual shift towards take-overs would be indicative of greater uncertainty in the aftermath of the collapse of the Bretton Woods system, the emergence of new competition, intensified pressure for structural change, etc. However, the growing emphasis on take-overs represents a trend which has long been present throughout the industrial spectrum.

Table 18 shows the advance of acquisitions across industries since the beginning of the twentieth century. While take-overs used to be most frequent in 'other industries' and in chemicals, the share was the largest in basic industries during the last decade. As operations were internationalized relatively late in this latter sector, acquisition was chosen as the major mode of entry from the

Table 17 Proportion of take-overs in the periods 1971–80 and 1981–90, by country, per cent

Country	1971–80	1981–90
Belgium	62	88
France	76	94
Italy	67	97
Netherlands	50	86
Germany	76	81
Denmark	68	89
United Kingdom	62	80
Ireland	20	100
Portugal	60	75
Spain	86	83
Greece	100	100
Austria	60	75
Finland	35	74
Norway	80	79
Switzerland	90	83
United States	63	77
Canada	67	55
Japan	25	33
Austria	38	78
New Zealand	0	100
Africa	100	100
Asia	43	46
Latin America	53	76

Source: IUI database

onset. Within engineering, machinery and transport had the greatest proportion of greenfield operations in the 1980s, still accounting for less than 30 per cent of the total.

It is true that deregulation and the liberalization of investment regimes have gradually facilitated the process of acquisition in many markets and industries. The systematic shift towards take-overs indicates that additional factors have been at work, however. This is further suggested by the variation in entry mode that remains across countries and industries (Andersson and Svensson, 1995).

Acquisitions are subject to certain conditions, including the availability of suitable objects for take-over. These do not have to be prosperous firms, but it has to be possible to adjust them in accordance with the objectives of the purchaser. On the other hand, high share prices make it expensive to buy firms, favouring

Table 18 Proportion of acquisitions among affiliates in different
industries and period of acquisition, 1901–90, per cent

Industry	1901–60	1961–70	1971–80	1981–90
Basic	4	44	69	92
Chemicals	30	33	52	80
Engineering	23	43	62	81
Metal products	0	21	68	85
Machinery	16	44	52	76
Electronics	10	61	65	87
Transport	20	50	40	78
Other industries	43	42	64	71
All industries	23	43	62	81

Source: IUI database

greenfield operations. The continuing integration of financial
markets reduces the extent to which 'national' prices matter, however. The surge of cross-border mergers and acquisitions in Europe in the late 1980s, for instance, was paralleled by rocketing
share prices.

As establishing a new firm takes more time than acquiring an
existing one, a great need for rapid success tends to favour take-
overs. Once a firm has established a local presence in a market,
additional affiliates are more likely to be established through take-
over in order to reduce rather than increase the competitive
pressure. More fundamentally, however, the choice between
greenfield operations and acquisition is determined by the needs
and abilities of the investing firm.

Broadly speaking, the two entry modes require somewhat different skills, the former being based on owner-specific technology
and the latter stimulated by the ability to organize technologies in
general. Thus a preference for take-overs reflects the capacity to
streamline and harmonize assets in separate organizations, thereby gaining advantages of synergy. Of course, in many instances
the objective behind an investment is not to enter a particular
market, but to acquire a certain, interesting potential partner firm.
Examining the variation in start-ups across firms over time, a high
degree of reliance on 'in-house technology', measured as R&D
intensity in the parent company, turns out to favour greenfield
operations. On the other hand, acquisition is favoured by a relatively heavy emphasis on organizational skill, measured by, e.g.,

the degree of experience of international operations. These considerations suggest that acquisition will remain the predominant entry mode in foreign markets (Andersson and Svensson, 1995).

In the following chapters, the significance of organizational factors is further examined in various contexts.

4

MULTINATIONAL COMPANIES AND TRADE

INTERNATIONAL TRADE IN TRANSITION

A very large proportion of world trade is today controlled by MNCs. More than three-quarters of total exports of goods, and as much as one-third of world exports, have been estimated to consist of intra-firm deliveries rather than transactions at arm's length (UNCTAD, 1994). Nevertheless, conventional trade theory has not paid much attention to MNCs. Trade was explained by comparative advantages, generated by inter-country differences in factor endowments and technology, while production factors were assumed more or less immobile with respect to national boundaries.

Through FDI, however, entire bundles of production factors, mostly excluding natural resources, have become much more geographically transferable. Moreover, in the most expansive sectors, production is characterized by the intensive use of endogenously determined assets, such as technology, trade marks and skills in the labour force. A great many of these are created and owned by MNCs, which, in principle, can apply them all over the world. Thus the localization decisions made by MNCs increasingly influence the international distribution of productive resources. Their actions may strengthen already existing trade patterns as well as create new ones.

Early studies of the impact of MNCs on international trade used FDI as a proxy for international production. Since FDI statistics measure investment rather than the value of output, however, they are likely to underestimate the magnitude of MNC activities. A more useful indicator of MNC operations is the value of affiliate sales. Unfortunately, few countries collect such information, hampering international comparisons.

Mainly owing to the scarcity of firm-level data, knowledge about the connection between foreign output and trade is still limited. It is widely accepted that local production and exports may be viewed as alternative means of serving foreign markets, but also that they often complement each other. The relationship between the two critically depends on the underlying reason for carrying out production in a country. For example, when foreign manufacturing is undertaken as a response to prevailing or expected trade barriers, resulting in horizontal expansion, it can be seen as substituting for trade. However, if the company would otherwise have been prohibited from selling on the host market, the local presence is not replacing exports but rather filling a gap. Meanwhile, when MNC activities are characterized by vertical interconnections and plant economies of scale, international production generally stimulates increased cross-border exchange.[1]

Connections between foreign production and trade have predominantly been analysed in a two-country framework, comprising a home and a host country (cf. Horst, 1973). The basic assumption has been that the headquarters serve as a node to which foreign activities are connected, and consequently that the affiliates' output is either sold locally, or exported back home. As noted in, e.g., UNCTAD (1993), MNCs have gradually developed into complex networks of integrated international production, and the output from foreign affiliates is to a great extent exported to third markets. Thus, in order to take full account of the scope of MNC operations and their impact on trade, it is necessary to consider third-country aspects.

In this chapter, particular attention is paid to the internal structure of MNCs and how organizational patterns influence international trade. In the next section, the role of MNCs in Swedish trade is discussed. The following one analyses the connections between organizational modes and intra-firm trade, distinguishing between separate product categories in internalized transactions. Geographical and sectoral variations in the links between MNC activities and trade are depicted in the fourth and fifth sections respectively. The sixth addresses the increase of take-overs as an entry mode when expanding in foreign markets, and investigates how it has affected trade between affiliates and parent companies. Incorporating third-country sales from foreign affiliates in the analysis, the final section reviews the relationship between foreign production and home-country exports.

FOREIGN PRODUCTION AND EXPORTS BY SWEDISH MNCS

Table 19 shows that Swedish MNCs play a prominent role in the country's trade, controlling well over half of the total exports in goods.[2] Including firms with foreign sales affiliates but no production abroad, the share increased to 58 per cent in 1990 (see note to Table 19). With regard to affiliates of foreign-owned MNCs, their contribution to Swedish exports rose from 7 per cent to 23 per cent between 1970 and 1991. As of the early 1990s, the share of exports accounted for by MNCs was thus likely to exceed 80 per cent, which is similar to observations for other major home countries of MNCs, such as the United States and the United Kingdom (UNCTC, 1988; UN, 1991).[3]

Table 19 Total Swedish exports and exports accounted for by parent companies of Swedish MNCs, selected years 1970–91, current prices, SEK million and per cent

Measure	1970	1974	1978	1986	1990	1991
Total Swedish exports (ISIC 2 and 3)	33,930	68,140	94,800	260,330	331,160	326,210
Exports from parent companies						
SEK million	19,500	38,510	57,410	148,190	172,254	—
As percentage of total Swedish exports	57	57	61	57	52	—
Exports from foreign affiliates in Sweden						
SEK million	2,440	—	—	34,010	—	73,570
As percentage of total Swedish exports	7	—	—	13	—	23
Total share of FDI-related exports	64	—	—	70	—	—

Note: The figures presented for parent company exports include only the 119 MNCs with manufacturing affiliates abroad. If parent companies with foreign sales affiliates are added, total exports from parent companies in 1990 rise to SEK 190,915 million, which corresponds to 58 per cent of total Swedish exports.
Sources: Statistics Sweden, IUI, Andersson and Fredriksson (1993) and Samuelsson (1977)

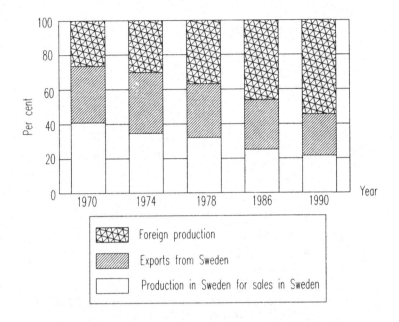

Figure 4 Distribution of Swedish MNCs' output and sales in Sweden
and abroad, selected years 1970–90, per cent
Source: IUI database

In Figure 4 the output of Swedish MNCs is divided into home-country manufacturing for local sales, exports from home, and foreign manufacturing. In 1970, some 75 per cent of total output was produced by the parents, and the home market absorbed 40 per cent of sales. Since then, the significance of both production and sales in Sweden has gradually declined, reaching only about 40 per cent and 20 per cent respectively in 1990.

Meanwhile, home-country operations have become more export-oriented. In 1990, 56 per cent of the Swedish output was shipped overseas, compared with 44 per cent in 1970.[4] Nevertheless, exports from the parent companies constitute a declining share of worldwide sales by Swedish MNCs. As can be seen in Figure 4, the proportion was relatively stable at about 33 per cent between 1970 and 1978. Since then, the share of parent exports has fallen gradually to about one-quarter in 1990. The decline was particularly pronounced in the late 1980s.

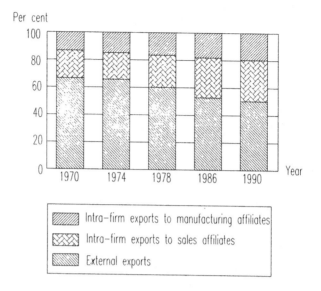

Figure 5 Composition of exports from parent companies of Swedish
MNCs, selected years 1970–90, per cent
Source: IUI database

Parallel to the expansion of manufacturing abroad, the composition of parent exports has changed. Above all, intra-firm
deliveries have become more important. As can be seen in Figure 5,
the share of parent exports that was sold to affiliated outlets increased
from one-third in 1970 to more than 50 per cent in 1990. The bulk of
intra-firm exports is channelled to sales affiliates, but manufacturing
affiliates have been the destination for a growing share, corresponding to about 20 per cent of total parent exports in 1990.

Despite the growth of intra-firm deliveries in parent exports,
manufacturing affiliates abroad have typically become less dependent on supplies from the home country. Figure 6 shows that
the ratio of imports from parent companies to the affiliates' total
sales declined from about 17 per cent in 1974 to 11 per cent in
1990. A growing number of manufacturing affiliates do not import
at all from the parent company.

At the same time, Figure 6 shows that manufacturing affiliates of
Swedish MNCs have become more export-oriented. In 1990,
foreign affiliate exports amounted to about half the volume of total
parent exports, a dramatic increase from 1986 when the corres-

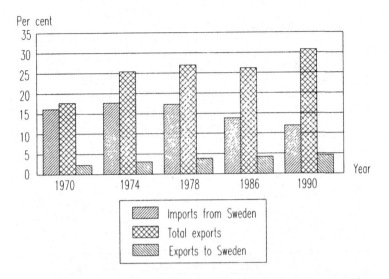

Figure 6 Imports from parent companies, total exports and exports to Sweden by manufacturing affiliates of Swedish MNCs in relation to the affiliates' total sales, selected years 1970–90, per cent
Source: IUI database

ponding figure was about one-third.[5] Between 1970 and 1990 affiliate exports almost doubled, from 17 per cent to 31 per cent of sales. Exports back home also increased, albeit from a low level. Compared with American and Japanese majority-owned affiliates, Swedish subsidiaries export a relatively large amount to third countries (see Figure 7). Regarding Japanese- and United States-owned affiliates, deliveries back home accounted for about 45 and 33 per cent of total exports respectively. In contrast, no more than 16 per cent of the Swedish-owned affiliates' exports went back home. This is in line with the smaller size of the home market. As will be discussed below, the adoption of different strategies in the internationalization process has also affected the tendency to export.

To summarize, while MNCs have become more important for Swedish exports, the share accounted for by Swedish-owned firms fell in the late 1980s. A growing part of the Swedish parent company output is channelled to foreign affiliates. From the manufacturing affiliates' perspective, however, trade with Sweden accounts for a shrinking share of total operations. In accordance with the relatively small size of the home country, Swedish-owned

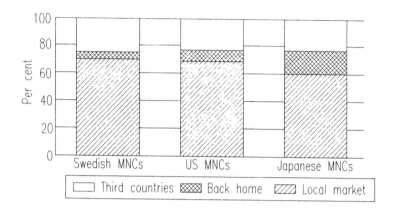

Figure 7 Destination of sales by Swedish, United States and Japanese
majority-owned affiliates abroad, 1990, per cent
Sources: Encarnation (1993); IUI database

affiliates export extensively to third countries compared with their
American and Japanese counterparts.

ORGANIZATIONAL MODES AND
INTRA-FIRM TRADE

Although the growth of intra-firm trade has attracted increased
attention, there is still scanty evidence on what determines the
choice between trading at arm's length and within organizations.
In Chapter 2 it was noted that explanations of intra-firm trade are
mostly based on theories of vertical integration (Williamson, 1971,
1979; Casson and associates, 1986). Consequently, the growth of
intra-firm trade in world exports has been interpreted as an expansion of vertically organized MNCs (UNCTAD, 1993).

At the same time, FDI among developed economies has been
argued to indicate the growing importance of market-proximity
considerations and horizontal expansion (Markuson, 1994;
Brainard, 1994). Other empirical results speak against a clear-cut
relationship between vertical integration and intra-firm trade.
Cho (1990) concluded that vertical integration does not have a
significant impact on the propensity of a product to be traded
internally. Moreover, although the presence of vertically integ-

rated links may be expected to be stronger between countries with dissimilar factor proportions, Helleiner and Lavergne (1980) found that the relative importance of related-party trade is much greater in United States imports from the OECD than in United States imports from developing countries. Others have found that intra-firm trade is positively influenced by the need for after-sales services (Lall, 1978; Zejan, 1989), which are likely to be more closely related to horizontal expansion.

These seemingly contrasting results can partly be attributed to the (often implicit) assumption in empirical studies that intra-firm trade between affiliated manufacturing plants consists of inter-mediate products only (cf. Lall, 1978; Helleiner, 1979; Pearce, 1982; Zejan, 1989). It is not obvious that trade within firms should be interpreted in this way. When analysing the impact of foreign manufacturing on trade, i.e. not treating pure sales and distribution activities as parts of the value-added chain, it is appropriate to regard intermediate products as made up of raw materials and semi-processed goods only.[6] Figure 8 shows that a significant share of parent exports to Swedish-owned producing affiliates con-

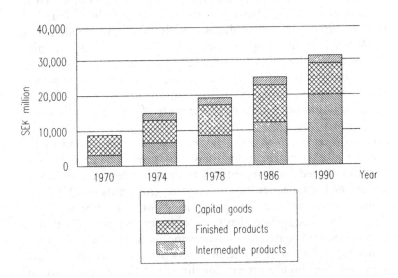

Figure 8 Composition of parent company exports to manufacturing affiliates of Swedish MNCs, identical firms, selected years 1970–90, fixed prices (base year 1990), SEK million
Source: IUI database

sists of finished goods, although the proportion fell in the late 1980s.[7]

Intra-firm trade in the two product types[8] has been claimed to be partly differently determined (Stubenitsky, 1970; Casson and associates, 1986). Furthermore, the composition of trade is likely to depend on the internal structure of the MNC. Trade in intermediates should be associated with economies of scale at the plant level, specialization of the value-added chain, i.e. vertical integration, and the exploitation of differences between countries in the conditions of production. Intra-firm trade in finished goods, on the other hand, is linked rather with horizontal expansion by the MNC where affiliates in different countries undertake similar production but import supplementary deliveries from the parent or from each other. This distinction is studied in Andersson and Fredriksson (1994a), where several characteristics of firms and countries are shown to be differently related to the propensity of affiliates to import the two product types.

The export intensity of the affiliate can be seen as a proxy for international specialization of production. The presence of economies of scale at the plant level and production in a relatively concentrated number of locations have both been found to favour exports from affiliates (Andersson and Fredriksson, 1994b). While intra-firm imports of intermediates are increasing in the export intensity of affiliates, the reverse is true of finished goods. Thus affiliates that primarily sell their output locally report relatively large intra-firm imports of goods for resale, which is in line with what can be expected for horizontally integrated units.

It has been noted that the nature of trade is influenced by the level of internationalization attained by firms. The propensity of Swedish-owned foreign affiliates to import intermediates as well as finished goods decreases as firms grow outside the home country. Making a similar observation for United States firms, Pearce (1982) suggested that trade between affiliates will replace trade between the parent company and its foreign subsidiaries as firms expand their international network. In essence, this presupposes that highly internationalized MNCs are vertically organized, with affiliates performing specialized operations in different countries.

However, in vertically organized MNCs where the parent company and its foreign affiliates perform highly specialized tasks and are mutually dependent on each other, an increase in foreign production could be expected to be paralleled by an expansion of earlier stages of the value-added chain in the home country as well. This would suggest that a relatively large proportion of foreign production should rather be conducive to the predominance of horizontal integration in MNCs, with less trade on the whole between affiliated parties. This line of reasoning is given empirical support in Andersson and Fredriksson (1994b), where the export propensity of affiliates is shown to be negatively related to the degree of internationalization of MNCs.

It has furthermore been noted that the presence of proprietary, intangible assets should stimulate internalization, as well functioning markets are normally lacking for such assets. Several studies at the industry level have established a positive connection between intra-firm trade and R&D intensity (cf. Lall, 1978; Helleiner and Lavergne, 1980). Analyses of Swedish MNCs show that this applies to both finished and intermediate products.[9]

Thus, making the distinction between intermediate and finished goods in intra-firm exports, we see that a high proportion of intra-firm trade need not be indicative of vertical integration of production. Rather, the two types of trade are internalized partly for different reasons and relate to the structure of firm operations in varying ways. The accurate indicator of vertical integration is not intra-firm trade in general but intra-firm trade in intermediates, specifically. With this background, let us analyse how the trade pattern of Swedish MNCs varies across regions.

GEOGRAPHICAL PATTERNS

As can be seen in Table 20, Europe is the main foreign destination of products manufactured in Sweden. In 1990, the EC and EFTA together received almost three-quarters of all Swedish exports of goods. The EFTA countries, however, received a relatively small proportion of exports from parent companies of Swedish MNCs. The geographical proximity of the Nordic countries has facilitated exports particularly from smaller domestic firms. Meanwhile, MNCs account for a relatively large proportion of exports to more distant regions, although the geographical pattern varies across sectors. MNCs in basic industries, which rely on access to immobile natural resources and are confronted with high trans-

Table 20 Exports from parent companies of Swedish MNCs and total Swedish exports, by industry and region, 1990, per cent

Region	Engineering	Chemicals	Basic	All Swedish MNCs	Total Swedish exports
EC	44	60	81	57	54
EFTA	12	17	9	12	19
North America	19	7	5	14	10
Other OECD countries	5	6	0	3	5
Developing countries	20	10	4	14	12
Total	100	100	100	100	100

Note: EC and EFTA comprise those countries which belonged to the respective organizations in 1990.
*Columns may not add up to exactly 100 due to rounding off.
Source: Statistics Sweden

port costs, focus heavily on European markets, whereas MNCs in engineering display a much more diverse pattern.

Swedish MNCs have pursued different strategies in order to expand sales in various regions and countries. One indication of this is the large variations in the extent to which goods are exported internally, as shown in Table 21. Notable deviations can be observed even within Europe. While almost a third of parent exports to the EC-6 went to manufacturing affiliates, the corresponding figure for EFTA was only 8 per cent.[10] Among developed countries, the greatest share of intra-firm trade is reported for 'other countries', i.e. mainly Japan, Australia and New Zealand. In these distant markets, a local presence appears particularly important for sales.

The extent to which affiliates in different regions have received internal supplies from the home country is reported in Table 22, with the distinction drawn between intermediate and finished products. In Europe, affiliates located in the EC are typically more dependent on supplies from home than those in EFTA, particularly with regard to intermediates. This suggests a relatively high degree of vertical integration between parent companies and EC affiliates, while subsidiaries in EFTA are predominantly horizontally related to operations in the home country. In North America, deliveries of intermediates from the parent corresponded to only 4 per cent of affiliate sales. The geographical distance from Sweden

Table 21 Total parent exports and exports to manufacturing affiliates of Swedish MNCs, by region, 1990, SEK million and per cent

Region	Parent exports	Exports to manufacturing affiliates	Exports to affiliates/total exports (per cent)
Developed countries	130,862	29,930	23
EC-12	86,066	22,428	26
EC-6	55,154	16,741	30
EC-3	24,384	4,268	18
EC-South	6,528	1,419	22
EFTA	17,893	1,424	8
North America	20,946	3,824	18
Other	5,957	2,254	38
Developing countries	16,644	2,477	15
Africa	2,215	3	0
Asia	10,966	836	8
Latin America	3,463	1,639	47
Total	147,506	32,407	22

Note: The table is based on the responses from 108 Swedish MNCs concerning the destination of their exports from Sweden on a country-to-country basis. The total figure for parent exports is about 13 per cent lower compared with Table 20. Exports to countries in Eastern Europe and the former Soviet Union are included in the total for developing countries.
Source: IUI database

as well as the size of the host market has favoured local production rather than exports from the home country. Subsidiaries in 'other developed countries' report a very high propensity to import finished goods as well as intermediates from Sweden.

Concerning the developing world, Swedish MNCs have chosen different strategies in Latin America and Asia, partly in response to varying trade policies. In Latin America, high barriers to trade have favoured tariff-jumping FDI and local manufacture rather than direct exports from the home country, while the reverse is true in the case of Asia. Although sales by Swedish-owned affiliates in 1990 were five times greater in Latin America than in Asia, parent exports to the former region corresponded to only one-third of exports to the latter. Moreover, almost 30 per cent of sales from Asian affiliates were provided by the parent company in 1990.

Table 22 Sales and imports from parents by foreign manufacturing affiliates of Swedish MNCs, by region, 1990, SEK million and per cent

Region	Sales (SEK million)	Imports from parent/sales (per cent)	Imports of intermediates /sales (per cent)	Imports of finished goods/sales (per cent)
Developed countries	282,997	12	8	4
EC-12	195,026	13	9	4
EC-6	138,115	13	9	4
EC-3	43,205	10	7	3
South-EC	13,706	10	7	3
EFTA	16,043	10	3	7
North America	62,636	7	4	3
Other developed countries	9,293	24	13	11
Developing countries	18,636	14	9	5
Africa	304	1	0	1
Asia	3,103	28	10	18
Latin America	15,229	11	8	3
Total*	301,633	12	7	5

Note:: *Columns may not add up exactly, due to rounding off.
Source: IUI database

Compared with United States and Japanese MNCs, Swedish firms have devoted relatively little attention to the developing world. In 1990, about 25 per cent of the total outward stock of Japanese and United States FDI was located outside the OECD (UN, 1992). The corresponding figure for Sweden was less than 8 per cent (Central Bank of Sweden, 1993). Furthermore, while Japanese and United States MNCs have established extensive off-shore production in low-income countries in order to export back home, Swedish manufacturing there has mainly served local markets. As can be seen in Table 23, Swedish-owned affiliates in developing countries exported only 9 per cent of their output in 1990. A negligible amount was shipped back to Sweden.

Affiliate exports are significantly higher in developed countries. The most export-oriented subsidiaries are found in Europe, and especially in the EC-6, where almost half of the output was

Table 23 Sales and exports from foreign manufacturing affiliates of
Swedish MNCs, by region, 1990, SEK million and per cent

Region	Sales	Exports	Exports to Sweden	Exports/ sales (per cent)	Exports to Sweden/ sales (per cent)
Developed countries	282,997	89,509	14,659	32	5
EC-12	195,026	75,599	12,488	39	6
EC-6	138,115	64,263	10,713	47	8
EC-3	43,205	8,933	1,418	21	3
EC-South	13,706	2,403	357	18	3
EFTA	16,043	5,293	1,156	33	7
North America	62,636	7,925	837	13	1
Other developed countries	9,293	692	178	7	2
Developing countries	18,636	1,619	333	9	2
Africa	304	0	0	0	0
Asia	3,103	83	8	3	0
Latin America	15,229	1,536	325	10	2
Total	301,633	91,128	14,991	31	5

Source: IUI database

exported in 1990. While affiliates located in these six economies
accounted for less than half of total sales by all Swedish-owned
affiliates, their share of exports exceeded 70 per cent. This situation is associated with the European integration process, which
has stimulated a more intense cross-border exchange within Europe and in the EC in particular. The export intensity of affiliates in
both EFTA and the EC increased in the late 1980s, suggesting
stronger international specialization of production in Europe. Thus,
although comprehensive information is lacking on the destination of
third-market exports, the bulk is likely to have been destined within
the same region as the host country. The propensity to export back
to Sweden was the highest in the EC-6 and in EFTA, and comprised
almost exclusively intra-firm deliveries to the parent.

With regard to non-European industrialized countries, the
export intensity of Swedish affiliates generally does not exceed 10

per cent of sales. As expected, however, Canada represents an exception, with more than 30 per cent of sales directed to third markets, most often the United States. Swedish affiliates in the United States doubled their export ratio at a low level from 5 per cent to 10 per cent of sales between 1986 and 1990. With NAFTA[11] in operation, affiliate exports from Canada and the United States are expected to increase further in the years ahead. The same should be true of affiliates located south of the Rio Grande. In 1990, Swedish plants in Mexico exported a meagre 4 per cent of their output.

Summing up, in contrast to observations of MNCs from large home countries, Swedish investments in the developing world have generally been motivated by market-proximity considerations, resulting in low levels of exports from affiliates. Owing to differences in trade policies, however, the choice between exporting from home and establishing foreign manufacturing varies between Asia and Latin America, with a considerably stronger local presence in the latter region. Within the developed countries, strong vertical links are present between parent companies and affiliates in the EC. Meanwhile, affiliates in EFTA are predominantly horizontally related to home-country operations. Exports from Swedish-owned affiliates are mainly accounted for by those located in the six original members of the EC. In North America, production is undertaken very much independently of the European parts of the MNC network. The affiliates in the United States display low import and export intensities.

SECTORAL PATTERNS

We have already noted that there are large sectoral variations in the geographical destination of exports. MNCs in basic industries are highly focused on European markets, while the distribution of exports of engineering products is considerably more diverse. In addition, there are important differences in the extent and nature of trade between parent companies and the foreign affiliates. As can be seen in Table 24, only 5 per cent of exports from parent companies in basic industries consisted of intra-firm deliveries to manufacturing affiliates, whereas the corresponding shares in chemicals and engineering were 15 per cent and 30 per cent respectively. Over time, the intra-firm constituent in parent exports has grown especially fast in the subsectors of engineering,

Table 24 Exports to foreign manufacturing affiliates as a share of total parent exports, by industry, 1970–90, per cent

Industry	1970	1974	1978	1986	1990
Basic	12.9	10.9	14.4	7.3	5.3
Chemicals	15.7	18.4	16.0	9.5	14.8
Engineering	14.6	18.4	20.8	20.3	29.8
Metal products	10.7	10.3	13.9	31.8	46.1
Machinery	23.5	20.6	25.5	26.2	22.3
Electronics	18.8	24.0	15.2	18.1	32.0
Transport	7.8	13.9	23.6	18.4	26.8
Total	12.7	14.0	16.9	16.5	20.1

Source: IUI database

while it has declined in basic industries. This is in line with the observation that intra-firm trade is increasing with the R&D intensity of firms.

As shown in Table 25, affiliates in transport are predominantly vertically integrated with the parent company.[12] The transport industry is characterized by global competition and economies of scale, stimulating the development of complex integration networks.[13] In 1990, intra-firm shipments from the home country amounted to as much as 30 per cent of affiliates' sales, and consisted almost exclusively of intermediates. In 1978, the corresponding figure was 36 per cent. Meanwhile, intra-firm trade in the opposite direction, i.e. from affiliates to parent companies has grown. Between 1978 and 1990, intra-firm exports to Sweden increased from 5 per cent to 20 per cent of the affiliates' sales. The presence of extensive two-way trade flows is typical not only of Swedish MNCs in transport but also of most other large car manufacturers such as Ford, General Motors, Toyota, etc. (UNCTAD, 1993).

Notable imports of intermediate products are reported for iron and steel as well. Compared with transport, however, affiliates in this industry obtain relatively large intra-firm deliveries of finished goods and export much less. This suggests that market-proximity considerations have been an important motive for expansion abroad and that foreign manufacturing relies to a relatively high degree on natural resources at home. Similar observations can be made of MNCs in the metal products industry, which is closely linked with the iron and steel sector in Sweden.

Table 25 Imports from parent company and exports by foreign manufacturing affiliates of Swedish MNCs relative to sales, by industry, 1990, SEK million and per cent

Industry	Sales	Imports of intermediate products/ sales (per cent)	Imports of finished goods/ sales (per cent)	Affiliates with no imports from parent, percent of all affiliates	Exports/ sales (per cent)	Exports to Sweden/ sales (per cent)
Basic industries	44,921	4	2	37	38	1
Pulp and paper	39,661	3	0	37	39	1
Iron and steel	5,260	10	12	38	28	1
Chemicals	30,282	6	2	32	16	3
Engineering	195,583	11	4	38	32	7
Metal products	35,718	4	10	20	23	2
Machinery	49,595	2	4	46	40	4
Electronics	69,368	7	5	48	19	3
Transport	40,902	28	2	15	56	20
Other industries	30,848	2	4	56	22	3
All industries	301,633	8	4	39	31	5

Source: IUI database

In paper and pulp, the dependence of affiliates on parent supplies fell rapidly in the late 1980s. At the same time, the export intensity escalated from about one-quarter to almost 40 per cent of affiliate sales. These developments were mainly an effect of the large acquisitions that were undertaken in the UK and Germany during the period. With only 5 per cent of parent exports channelled through manufacturing affiliates, foreign production has not been motivated by any immediate need to provide new market opportunities for parent exports. Rather, acquisitions have been part of a general strategy to increase the market share for the group of companies as a whole, and reduce the risk of discrimination from the EC, and as a response to increased demand for the use of recycled paper in the wake of growing environmental concern.

Electronics and machinery are the two largest industries in terms of foreign sales by manufacturing affiliates. As noted in Chapter 3, they are also the most internationalized sectors, with 75 per cent and 80 per cent of the total work force employed outside the home country. Foreign operations in both sectors are relatively independent of parent supplies. In fact, almost half of all foreign manufacturing affiliates in these industries import nothing at all from the parent company. Affiliates in electronics display a strong focus on production for the local market; less than 20 per cent of sales was exported in 1990. Together, these observations suggest that market-proximity factors have been the predominant reason for manufacturing abroad. In both these industries, an increase of intermediate product imports from the parent company in the late 1980s was paralleled by declining dependence on finished goods produced in Sweden.

It should be noted that the export intensity of affiliates increased in all industries except for the mixed group of 'other industries'. Furthermore, in all sectors except basic industries, the composition of parent exports to manufacturing affiliates abroad shifted from finished towards intermediate products. What this implies for the relationship between home and foreign operations will be returned to in Chapter 6.

INTRA-FIRM TRADE AND MODE OF ESTABLISHMENT

As discussed in Chapter 3, the expansion of MNC activities has increasingly been driven by large mergers and acquisitions in the industrialized economies. This applied not least to the surge of Swedish FDI in Europe in the late 1980s, when almost 90 per cent of all new establishments were acquired. For several reasons, the gradual shift away from greenfield investments is likely to affect the trade behaviour of MNCs, especially with regard to intra-firm transactions.

Through greenfield investments the MNC is able to tailor a foreign plant from the start so as to make it fit the existing production network. At the initial stage, a new venture is likely to be strongly dependent on the parent company in terms of both technology and supplies of input goods. In contrast, when it acquires an existing company, the MNC has to adapt ongoing operations to a prevailing network of customer and supplier relations, which may take time to integrate with the new parent company. Consequently, new ventures can be expected to be more inclined to

Table 26 Propensity of Swedish-owned affiliates to import from parent, and the proportion of intermediates in their overall imports, by entry mode, selected years 1970–90, per cent

Measure	1970	1974	1978	1986	1990
Greenfield venture					
Total imports from parent/sales	19.8	21.0	21.5	20.3	20.0
Share of intermediate products	35	44	46	53	78
Proportion of affiliates with no imports from parent	–	18	11	16	19
Acquisition					
Total imports from parent/sales	7.6	10.1	10.4	7.3	7.0
Share of intermediate products	53	59	66	52	63
Proportion of affiliates with no imports from parent	–	28	30	38	47

Source: IUI database

import from the home country, at least in a short-term perspective, than those established through acquisition.

A negative relationship between acquisition as mode of entry and the propensity to import from the parent has also been established in multiple regression analysis at the level of individual affiliates (Zejan, 1989). As shown in Andersson and Fredriksson (1994a), this applies to imports of both intermediate and finished products. There does not seem to be any systematic deviation in the export behaviour of acquisitions and greenfield start-ups, however.

In Table 26, the trade pattern of Swedish-owned foreign manufacturing affiliates is depicted by mode of entry. Affiliates established through greenfield investments report total imports from the parent company amounting to approximately 20 per cent of their sales. As expected, the import intensity is considerably lower in acquired affiliates. The shares have been relatively constant between 1970 and 1990 for the two groups of affiliates. In the case of greenfield investments, however, there has been a gradual shift in the composition of imports. The share of intermediates has increased from 35 per cent to 78 per cent of the total during the observed period, with the greatest change occurring in the late 1980s. A possible interpretation is that late stages in the value-added chain have been reallocated from parent companies to greenfield affiliates abroad, resulting in enhanced intra-firm exports of intermediate products from the former.[14] In the case of acquisitions, on the other hand, a growing proportion of all affiliates, reaching almost 50 per cent in 1990, are totally independent of supplies from the parent.

It is not possible on the basis of the information presented in Table 26 to say anything about the long-term connection between entry modes and trade between parents and affiliates. In fact, whether the observed discrepancies in import behaviour tend to disappear in the longer run has never been empirically examined. It may be expected that acquired subsidiaries will become more integrated with the rest of an MNC in time, and that previous supplier relations will be abandoned in favour of internal inputs from the parent company, in order to harmonize purchases and reap economies of scale at the corporate level. A similar but converse argument can be put forward regarding greenfield affiliates, as an initially heavy dependence on parent supplies may weaken when contacts are developed with local subcontractors. If that is the case, the import pattern of the two entry modes should converge over time.

This proposition can be examined by tracing the behaviour of individual affiliates over time. Using the IUI data, it is possible to follow two groups of affiliates over the periods 1965–86 and 1974–90. The first sample consists of 33 subsidiaries established between 1955 and 1965, of which 21 were new ventures and 12 were acquired (Table 27). The second group comprises 44 outlets, all of which were started between 1964 and 1974. In this case, there are 17 greenfield ventures and 27 acquisitions (Table 28). A natural hypothesis is that the import dependence of the two groups of affiliates tends to converge over time, from a situation where greenfield investments initially have relatively large imports from the parent company. Using a one-sided T test, the arithmetic means of the two samples are compared to determine whether they differ significantly from each other. A distinction is made between intermediate and finished goods.

As can be seen from Table 28, the arithmetic means reported in 1974 were considerably higher for greenfield start-ups than for acquisitions. This applied to total imports as well as to imports of intermediate and finished goods. In 1990, the difference had disappeared. Nevertheless, owing to very large variations within each subgroup the respective means cannot be distinguished from each other statistically, either in 1974 or in 1990.[15] However, in the case

Table 27 Imports from parent companies as a proportion of sales by affiliates established between 1955 and 1965, arithmetic means, by means of entry, selected years 1965–86, per cent

Year	Total imports from parent/sales		Imports of intermediates/sales		Imports of finished goods/sale	
	Green -field	Acquisition	Green -field	Acquisition	Green -field	Acquisition
1965	33.3**	6.9**	11.2*	4.2*	22.1**	1.0**
1970	24.5**	6.6**	11.0	5.6	13.4**	0.5**
1974	21.1	12.6	14.0	8.8	6.9	3.7
1978	22.4**	8.6**	13.7**	5.6**	9.0*	2.9*
1986	18.4	9.3	11.6**	4.5**	6.8	4.4

Note: The sample consists of 21 greenfield ventures and 12 acquired affiliates. ** and * indicate that the difference between the two means is statistically significant at the 5 and 10 per cent levels respectively.
Source: IUI database

of intermediates, the groups diverged from each other up to 1986, when the arithmetic mean of acquired subsidiaries was significantly lower than that of greenfield investments.

Returning to Table 27, the convergence hypothesis can be rejected with regard to imports of intermediates. The discrepancy is actually more significant at the end of the period studied. While the difference between greenfield ventures and acquisitions is statistically certain only at the 10 per cent level in 1965, it is significant at the 5 per cent level in 1978 and 1986. Meanwhile, the

Table 28 Imports from parent companies as a proportion of sales by affiliates established between 1964 and 1974, arithmetic means, by mode of entry, selected years 1974–90, per cent

Year	Total imports from parent/sales		Imports of intermediates/sales		Imports of finished goods/sales	
	Green- field	Acquisition	Green- field	Acquisition	Green- field	Acquisition
1974	55.5	17.7	32.3	13.8	14.1	4.9
1978	27.3*	16.8*	19.3	11.8	8.4	4.6
1986	21.3	13.9	15.9*	8.1*	5.3	7.0
1990	14.4	13.7	9.2	10.2	4.5	4.8

Note: The sample consists of 17 greenfield ventures and 27 acquired affiliates. ** and * indicate that the difference between the two means is statistically significant at the 5 and 10 per cent levels respectively.
Source: IUI database

reverse trend can be observed in the case of finished goods, as the difference in import behaviour that was discernible in 1965 had been eliminated by 1986.

It is worth noting that the observed convergence with regard to finished goods is explained mainly by declining imports in greenfield affiliates, rather than by growing dependence on parent company supplies in acquired subsidiaries. In fact, in no column of Tables 27 and 28 is there a large increase in the import intensity of the latter group of affiliates. This may be due to difficulties in changing the prevailing supplier structure of acquired companies. Alternatively, the MNC may have had no intention of expanding intra-firm exports from the home country.

The fact that the hypothesis of convergence was rejected in the case of intermediates suggests that greenfield investments are preferred when vertical links are desired between the new venture and the parent company. This is in line with the finding in Chapter 3 that heavy reliance on 'in-house technology' tends to favour greenfield operations. Meanwhile, the large number of affiliates which have no trade with the parent company suggests that other motives have dominated in the case of acquisitions.

PRODUCTION IN AFFILIATES AND HOME COUNTRY EXPORTS

From the preceding sections it is clear that the connections between international production and trade vary, depending on the reasons for expanding beyond the boundaries of the home country. Whether production abroad complements or substitutes for exports from the home country provides one important indication of how foreign operations affect domestic activities, including the economic performance of the host country.

When a foreign manufacturing affiliate is established, home country exports may be affected in several ways. The affiliate's output can be expected to replace that part of the parent company's exports of finished goods which was previously sent to the host country. However, if exporting from the home country is not an option, e.g. owing to high transport costs or prohibitive tariffs, local production is not replacing trade but rather filling a gap. At the same time, there is a potentially complementary impact in so far as the affiliates use intermediate goods produced by the parent

69

company, which applies in the case of vertical integration, or by other firms in the home country.

The question of how the MNCs' expansion abroad has impinged on economic performance in the home country has been given plentiful attention, particularly in the United States and Sweden. Historically, both their economies were characterized by much larger outflows than inflows of FDI. Bergsten *et al.* (1978) found that foreign sales by affiliates of United States MNCs boosted the home country's exports up to a certain point. At even higher levels of internationalization, however, home country exports were found to be replaced by manufacturing abroad. Judging from case studies, Jordan and Vahlne (1981) concluded that the establishment of foreign manufacturing affiliates led to larger market shares for Swedish companies and greater exports of intermediate products from home. Using cross-section firm-level data, Swedenborg (1979, 1982) similarly concluded that an increase in foreign manufacturing on average led to a positive marginal effect on home country exports. On the basis of analyses at the industry level, Lipsey and Weiss (1981, 1984) and Blomström *et al.* (1988) likewise rejected the hypothesis of a negative relationship between foreign production and exports from the home country.

Thus most studies have found zero or positive effects from overseas production on home country exports. The findings referred to above are based almost exclusively on data concerning the 1960s and the 1970s, however. The dramatic changes in the operations of MNCs that have already been observed in this book make it a matter of particular interest to reconsider the connection between the expansion of foreign production and Swedish exports in the 1980s.

Table 29 shows what proportion of affiliates has imported intermediates from the parent company. In 1974, almost 60 per cent of all manufacturing units abroad relied to varying degrees on intra-firm inputs from the home country. Whereas this share remained stable until 1978, it fell sharply to 43 per cent in 1986 and to 37 per cent in 1990. A similar development can be seen in all regions. This means that the positive impact of an incremental increase in foreign production on intra-firm exports from Sweden should have been considerably smaller than in previous decades.

Table 30 depicts how the output from foreign affiliates has developed in different regions as a share of total foreign sales of

Table 29 Proportion of Swedish-owned foreign manufacturing affiliates which imported intermediate products from the parent company, by region, 1974–90, per cent

Region	1974	1978	1986	1990
EC-6	55	56	43	33
EC-3	71	53	51	40
EC-South	48	52	36	37
EFTA	53	47	30	41
North America	68	73	38	32
Other developed countries	63	76	67	52
Developing countries	62	67	47	43
All regions	59	58	43	37

Source: IUI database

'Swedish' goods.[16] An increase indicates that exports from Sweden account for a shrinking proportion of total foreign sales in a region. Between 1965 and 1974, manufacturing affiliates accounted for 28 per cent of total foreign sales of Swedish goods. By 1978 this share had increased to 34 per cent, as shifts in favour of local manufacturing were observed in all developed regions. From 1978 to 1986, Swedish exports grew at approximately the same rate as local manufacturing in most regions, with the exceptions of

Table 30 Percentage of Swedish total foreign sales produced abroad, by region, selected years 1965–90.

Region	1965	1970	1974	1978	1986	1990
EC-12	27	32	32	39	39	47
EC-6	35	42	43	47	46	51
EC-3	14	15	14	22	24	38
EC-South	8	26	26	36	42	50
EFTA	13	12	11	15	17	18
North America	47	37	38	46	57	63
Other DCs	27	32	31	37	38	34
Africa	9	5	6	1	1	5
Asia	38	27	14	6	10	9
Latin America	42	49	46	65	62	67
All regions	27	29	28	34	38	45

Note: Foreign sales include *total Swedish exports of goods* (excluding trade with Eastern Europe) plus *sales by all foreign manufacturing affiliates* of Swedish-owned MNCs less intra-firm deliveries from the parent companies to those affiliates.
Source: IUI database and Statistics Sweden

North America and EC-South. In the latter half of the 1980s, the rapid expansion abroad led to a dramatic increase in the local manufacturing share, particularly in the EC.

At the same time, manufacturing affiliates in the EC became more important as exporters. While their exports corresponded to 24 per cent of total Swedish exports to the EC in 1978, this ratio had risen to 41 per cent by the end of the 1980s. Table 31 reports the development of Swedish exports compared to world and OECD exports. Between 1970 and 1992, Sweden's share fell from 2.4 per cent to 1.5 per cent of world exports. Relative to the OECD, the decline was even more accentuated.[17] There was a certain recovery in the first half of the 1980s, primarily as an effect of successive devaluations of the Swedish krona. From 1986 to 1992, however, the Swedish share of world exports dropped from 1.9 per cent to 1.5 per cent. Swedish MNCs, on the other hand, defended their share in the period 1974–90.[18] As can be seen from the table, this strong performance is entirely explained by the expansion of affiliate exports. While the parents' share of world exports fell from 1.2 per cent to 0.9 per cent, that of Swedish-owned manufacturing affiliates more than doubled, with the fastest rise occurring in the late 1980s.

Table 31 Share of Sweden and of Swedish MNCs in world and OECD exports, selected years 1970–92, per cent

Measure	1970	1974	1978	1982	1986	1990	1992
Swedish exports' share of:							
World exports	2.4	2.1	1.8	1.6	1.9	1.7	1.5
OECD exports	3.3	3.2	2.5	2.3	2.6	2.3	2.1
Swedish MNCs' share of:							
World exports	1.6	1.4	1.4	n.a.	1.4	1.4	n.a.
OECD exports	2.2	2.2	1.9	n.a.	2.0	1.9	n.a.
Swedish parent exports as a share of:							
World exports	1.4	1.2	1.1	n.a.	1.1	0.9	n.a.
OECD exports	1.9	1.9	1.5	n.a.	1.5	1.2	n.a.
Foreign affiliates' share of:							
World exports	0.2	0.2	0.3	n.a.	0.3	0.5	n.a.
OECD exports	0.3	0.3	0.4	n.a.	0.5	0.7	n.a.

Source: IMF (various issues) and IUI database

Taken together, these observations suggest that the foreign operations of Swedish MNCs, particularly in the EC, were less complementary to operations in the home country than in previous periods. Similar conclusions have been drawn in recent econometric analyses at the firm level (Svensson, 1993, 1994). Compared with earlier empirical studies, these contributions differ in two main respects. First, the analyses cover all countries to which the parent company exports, i.e. not only those hosting manufacturing affiliates.[19] Second, to account for the fact that a strongly increased share of the affiliates' output is sold in third markets, a distinction is drawn between local sales and exports from affiliates.[20] Particularly in the EC, the affiliates' exports to third countries may substitute for exports from the parent company, unless a dissimilar range of products is manufactured in the EC plants from those in the parent company. In order to examine this proposition, exports from affiliates located in the EC are related to:

1 Parent exports of finished goods to the EC outside the host country of the manufacturing affiliate.
2 Parent exports of intermediate goods to the country in which production takes place.

Contrasting with results obtained in earlier studies, the statistical examination of the period 1974–90 shows that an increase in complementary deliveries of intermediates did not fully compensate for the decline in parent exports of finished goods which arose with foreign production. The outcome critically depends on whether foreign output is sold locally or exported to third countries. An increase in *local* sales is associated with a rise in parent exports of intermediate products as well as a reduction of parent exports of finished goods to the same country. Although both effects are significant on their own, the net outcome is insignificant, and the size of the effects is relatively small. Concerning *export* sales from affiliates in the EC and parent exports, there is a negative and significant impact on the latter, i.e. the substitution effect is not outweighed by complementary supplies.

In his model, Svensson (1993) normalizes export flows and foreign output with the total sales of the MNC. Lipsey (1994) and Blomström and Kokko (1994) suggest that expansion of foreign production would raise total sales and consequently reduce the ratio of parent exports, even if the absolute value of parent exports is unchanged. However, as affiliate production in, and parent exports to, a specific country constitute a small fraction of the MNC's total sales, this counter-argument is of limited relevance. As shown in Svensson (1994), similar results are obtained when using the MNC's sales in the home country as denominator. In both models, the net effect on parent exports is negative but not statistically significant with regard to local sales, and strongly negative for export sales.

It may be suggested that taking into consideration supplies from unaffiliated subcontractors might improve the relationship between foreign production and home country exports since the suppliers may be induced to deliver to foreign units. Although it is difficult to investigate the matter adequately, there is not much evidence in that direction. According to Braunerhjelm (1991), for instance, Swedish MNCs tended to replace domestic subcontractors with foreign ones when new subsidiaries were established abroad during the 1980s. As can be seen from Table 30, the ratio of foreign output to total Swedish sales abroad increased rapidly in the late 1980s, even when total Swedish exports are included.

Furthermore, it should be noted that dependence on imported components in Swedish manufacturing has reduced the net contribution to the balance of payments from a given volume of exports, partly as an effect of rising exports from foreign affiliates back to Sweden. Imported parts and components are particularly important in engineering, whereas exports of raw material-based products still contain a relatively low degree of foreign inputs. Thus it is clear that the expansion of foreign production in the 1980s became less conductive to favourable impacts on the Swedish current account.

This does not mean that exports from Sweden would have been greater, or that the current account would have recorded a greater surplus, if firms had been prohibited from investing abroad. On the contrary, as has already been stressed, foreign manufacturing may be essential for a firm to remain competitive on the world market. It also appears natural that the ratio of foreign production to home country exports increases as firms based in a small economy expand worldwide. Such expansion is likely to be particularly pivotal for the adoption and development of modern technology. At the same time, one cannot equally sanguinely dismiss observations of a weakening industrial record at home. Rather than focusing on FDI as such, however, attention should be paid to the underlying causes which determine the connections between FDI and performance in terms of trade, growth or productivity. Apparently, the conditions for industrial activities in the 1980s were such that the Swedish MNCs chose to expand abroad instead of at home. This issue will be returned to in Chapter 6 as the connection between European integration and FDI is examined.

5

TECHNOLOGY AND MULTINATIONALS

A CRUCIAL FACTOR

The restructuring of MNCs across national borders influences resource allocation and welfare mainly through international transfers of the knowledge that is unique to their organizations. This knowledge is closely associated with technology, which determines how effectively capital, labour, natural resources and other factors of production are used. In addition, technological progress determines future opportunities through efficiency improvements in existing processes as well as the opening up of new areas of economic activity.

Of course, technology itself is a concept which is difficult to observe and evaluate. Nowadays, it is generally defined in a broad way: it includes capabilities in respect of products and processes as well as skills in services such as management and distribution. Technology may be divided into 'hardware', in the form of machines, equipment, tools and other objects, and 'software', which comprises personnel, manuals, organizational forms and so forth.

No available indicator, including research and development (R&D), patents, royalties, licence fees, equipment or training expenditure, is able to measure more than parts of the concept. Still, the development and application of technology has become an increasingly decisive factor in determining the competitiveness of firms and countries. Technology is not exogenously determined, but draws heavily on the efforts of institutions and individuals. Efforts are motivated by expectations that the investor will be able to exploit an innovation before others do, whereas the social benefits partly hinge on the speed with which it is diffused to others.

Activities which aim at the creation of industrial knowledge can broadly be referred to as R&D. The bulk of R&D is undertaken by private firms, although public research programmes, universities and other institutions play an important role. A range of activities may be included, stretching from interdisciplinary studies to the upgrading of work processes and products. Measuring R&D is normally a question of determining how substantial monetary resources are spent. The outcome of R&D is critically dependent on human skills and ideas, however, not only in its immediate exploitation but also as regards further applications.

In spite of the scarcity of data, and measurement problems, it is widely accepted that MNCs play a crucial role in both the development and the diffusion of technology. There is a need of more hard data and careful analysis of what determines the linkages. Measuring and interpreting data relating to technology and how it influences companies are associated with considerable difficulties at the aggregate level of countries and industries. With knowledge assets specific to companies, meaningful studies must take individual firm data into account. However, owing to the strategic importance of technology, firms are generally unwilling to reveal details about research activities and how they affect operations.

As mentioned in previous chapters, MNCs based in small, open economies may encounter certain specific challenges. For example, a relatively small home economy makes success in foreign markets particularly important for achieving economies of scale. With a number of large MNCs concentrating R&D in the home country, there may be a strong prevalence of favourable external effects as local knowledge is upgraded. There is not necessarily any conflict in this with the need to internationalize the process of knowledge creation, since the existence of a strong local research base is commonly a prerequisite of the capacity to absorb information from global networks. At the same time, rising competition for available resources, e.g. in the form of trained personnel may lead to rising costs, and the more so the weaker the response of the supply side.

In this chapter, we undertake an extensive mapping of data on research activities by Swedish MNCs, analysing driving forces as well as the consequences of observed developments. Some issues of general interest are raised. To what extent can greater expenditure on R&D explain success in MNCs' penetration of foreign markets, and how does firm organization influence R&D? How can transfers of knowledge be measured, and what is the role of R&D undertaken in the home country and in foreign affiliates respectively? What linkage, if any, is there between R&D and investment in human capital?

The chapter is organized as follows. R&D and technology indicators are surveyed in the next section for a number of OECD countries. Changes and patterns in the technology creation of Swedish MNCs between 1970 and 1990 are reported in the following section. The internationalization of R&D is then studied, while the fifth section explores connections between R&D and international competitiveness. Forces shaping technology transfers are subsequently examined, and finally we explore linkages between technology and human resource management, particularly in the form of training expenditures.

R&D AND TECHNICAL PROGRESS

The increased importance of technology and knowledge creation shows up in a number of ways. For example, there is an overwhelming expansion of output, investment and trade in industries which draw heavily on modern equipment and trained personnel relative to those which rather rely on natural resources, cheap labour and mature technologies. New areas are also being subjected to stiffening competition based on high knowledge content. The growth of R&D expenditure accounts for another concrete indication. Looking at trends since the 1970s, gross domestic expenditure on R&D (GERD) has grown faster than GDP in almost all OECD countries.[1] For the OECD as a whole, R&D intensity (comparing with national output) amounted to 1.8 per cent and 2.3 per cent in 1977 and 1985 respectively. Manufacturing accounted for the largest part, about two-thirds, of R&D carried out in the OECD. In terms of financing R&D, however, industry accounted for only 57 per cent. The difference essentially consisted of public financing (UN, 1992; OECD, 1989).

R&D expenditures have historically been concentrated in the largest industrial countries. In 1985, the 'Group of Seven' OECD countries (G-7) accounted for 91 per cent of total R&D expenditures in the OECD area, but only 84 per cent of total GDP. It

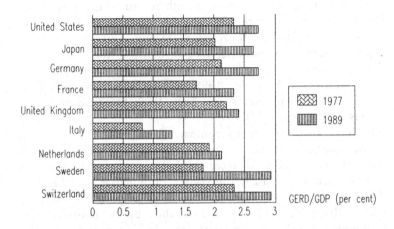

Figure 9 Gross domestic expenditure on R&D (GERD) as a percentage
of GDP in selected OECD countries, 1977 and 1989, per cent
Note: 1986 figure instead of 1989 for Switzerland; 1988 instead of 1989
for the United Kingdom
Sources: OECD (1989); United Nations (1992)

may be noted that the corresponding figure for the stock of outward FDI was 76 per cent. Still, as of the late 1980s, R&D intensity
exceeded 2 per cent of GDP in a great number of OECD countries. Figure 9 shows that Sweden, Switzerland, Germany, the
United States and Japan were at the top of the list. Thus among
those which devoted most resources to technological progress in
relative terms were small, highly trade-dependent economies as
well as the largest ones.[2]

As R&D generally is undertaken and financed by private
companies, the outcome should be expected to show up in firm
performance. Broadly speaking, one may identify two ways in
which R&D affects the performance of a firm:

1 Upgrading of technology in the form of process innovation
  yields greater output from any given combination of inputs, i.e.
  process innovation increases productivity.
2 New technology in the form of product innovation, or improvements in the quality of existing products, may result in
  higher value added and greater competitiveness.

It is well known that there may be a partial trade-off in the way technology creation is organized with regard to the purpose of improving existing work processes or products, or developing new ones. In either case, however, R&D aims at granting a firm an edge *vis-à-vis* its competitors. Several empirical studies have verified a significant impact of R&D on productivity and profitability (cf. Mairesse and Sassenou, 1991). Others have demonstrated a connection with market share (Lall, 1980; Swedenborg, 1982; Kravis and Lipsey, 1992).

It may be interesting to compare R&D, which serves as a measure of firms' efforts to create or upgrade technology, with a more direct indicator of technological output. Patent statistics represent one candidate in this context, although it is well known that patents may serve primarily as a strategic instrument. Of course, the return on R&D need not show up in patents, and the economic pay-off may also vary a great deal between patents. For instance, patents may cover parts of the output in terms of new products, but are probably less important in process development. While Table 32 shows that the number of national patent applica-

Table 32 Gross domestic expenditure on R&D (GERD) and number of national patent applications, 1985, plus annual real growth (per cent) in these variables, in selected OECD countries, 1975–85

| | 1985 | | Annual percentage real growth 1975–85[a] in | |
Country	GERD ($ million)	Number of national patent applications	GERD	Patents
United States	109,730	121,188	5.0	1.8
Japan	40,064	305,345	8.0	6.7
EC	63,849	320,176	4.0	3.3
Germany	19,774	75,231	3.8	3.0
France	14,571	54,766	4.7	3.1
United Kingdom	14,359	67,953	2.5	2.4
Italy	7,014	38,427	6.1	4.8
Netherlands	3,446	30,634	2.2	7.2
Sweden	2,946	29,571	7.4	7.2
Total OECD	230,901	895,068	5.0	4.3

a 1981–85 instead of 1975–85 for Germany.
Source: OECD (1989)

tions (domestic applications and applications by foreigners) grew somewhat less rapidly than industrial R&D expenditure in most OECD countries between 1975 and 1985, it still points towards a certain connection between the two. Below, this will be further considered at the firm level.

Keeping in mind the differences in patent regulations across countries, it may still be noted that domestic patent applications have increased very slowly worldwide; the growth which has come about is generally due to applications by foreigners. In the United States, foreign-owned firms accounted for almost 40 per cent of all applications in 1990, compared with about 30 per cent in the early 1980s. Furthermore, applications by foreigners have generally been more frequently accepted than domestic ones (OECD, 1989). This brings us back to the internationalization of technology.

TECHNOLOGY CREATION IN SWEDISH MNCS

Costs and benefits associated with technology are extremely difficult to specify and control through formal contracts, raising barriers to market transactions and putting large firms in a relatively advantageous position with regard to R&D. While MNCs have been found to account for the bulk of industrial R&D in the world economy, their dominance in technology creation is particularly conspicuous in certain small economies.

In the case of Sweden, MNCs generally base their competitiveness either on production factors which are specific to the home country, such as raw materials, or on technological assets. Altogether, Swedish MNCs spent nearly SEK 25 billion on R&D in 1990, as shown in Table 33. About 80 percent, SEK 20 billion, was undertaken in Sweden, compared with SEK 24 billion for the entire manufacturing sector of the country as of 1990. Thus Swedish MNCs dominate aggregate R&D activity in their home country. Moreover, the 20 largest Swedish MNCs, in respect of turnover, accounted for 97 per cent of aggregate R&D undertaken by the group of 116 MNCs in Sweden, and about the same proportion of R&D undertaken abroad. As of 1990, 20 out of 116 Swedish MNCs reported zero R&D expenditure.[3] These firms were small in terms of number of employees, and had only a small share of total employment located abroad when compared with MNCs which undertake R&D.

Table 33 R&D expenditure of Swedish MNCs, by industry, 1970–90, constant 1990 prices (SEK million)

| Industry | Total | | | | | Swedish | Foreign |
	1970	1974	1978	1986	1990	1990	
Basic	737	964	926	450	1,351	1,013	338
Chemicals	736	723	1,274	3,572	4,753	3,946	807
Other	898	715	895	576	265	162	103
Engineering	3,732	5,176	5,911	18,079	18,444	15,084	3,360
Metal products	75	90	105	733	876	689	187
Machinery	1,365	1,054	1,459	1,619	1,961	870	1,091
Electronics	1,667	2,288	2,453	6,703	6,070	4,524	1,546
Transport	625	1,744	1,894	9,024	9,537	9,001	536
All industries	6,103	7,578	9,006	22,677	24,813	20,205	4,608

Note: Different firms are included in an industry in different years, which may explain some jumps in R&D expenditures for some industries e.g. ASEA is included in electronics in 1986 but not in 1990.
Source: IUI database

The industrial distribution of R&D in Swedish MNCs is also reported in Table 33. Engineering accounted for almost 75 per cent by 1990. Two industries within engineering, transport and electronics, are together responsible for some 65 per cent of the total. In addition, substantial R&D activity is undertaken in the chemical industry, primarily in pharmaceuticals. Transport and chemicals have increased their shares particularly since the beginning of the 1970s. The industrial distribution resembles that in the OECD as a whole, where engineering and chemicals accounted for 66 per cent and 21 per cent respectively in 1983 (OECD, 1989).

In Figure 10 the average annual growth in real R&D expenditure is depicted between 1974 and 1990 for identical firms. A modest growth of about 4 per cent per annum on average between 1974 and 1978 was followed by almost 14 per cent annually between 1978 and 1986. In the late 1980s, the pace of growth slowed again, falling to some 5 per cent per year. While the changes are pronounced in the case of Swedish MNCs, the ups and downs coincide with those reported for the OECD as a whole. Between 1981 and 1985, GERD grew at an annual real rate of 6 per cent in OECD countries, on average,[4] and at approximately 4 per cent in 1986 and 1987 (OECD, 1989).

The overall growth is primarily driven by developments in engineering, which has been the largest R&D spender in Swedish

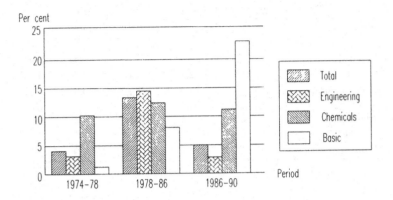

Figure 10 Average annual growth of R&D expenditure across industries, 1974–90, constant prices, per cent. The same firms are tracked in each group over each time period
Source: IUI database

industry throughout the period studied. Chemicals are the only industry which has recorded high and fairly stable growth in R&D expenditures during the entire period 1974–90, amounting to approximately 11 per cent per annum. The variation in basic industries should be interpreted with caution, given the very low initial level of R&D expenditures. Still, certain segments of basic industries became considerably more technology-intensive in the late 1980s. This appears to have been a matter both of catching up with competitors in some other European countries, such as Finland, and of the emergence of new high-technology niches within basic industries.

While absolute changes say little about the significance of R&D, a comparison with turnover provides a useful measure of firms' R&D intensity.[5] Table 34 shows that aggregate intensity rose from 2 per cent to 4 per cent for all firms from 1970 to 1990, with the steepest rise occurring between 1978 and 1986. The average level remained roughly constant in the late 1980s, although intensities actually increased in all three of the main industries. This is explained by the fact that basic industries, which had an overall intensity of only 1 percent, expanded most in these years in terms of turnover. Chemicals have demonstrated a high level throughout

Table 34 Total R&D intensity (total R&D/total turnover) of Swedish MNCs, by industry, selected years 1970–90, per cent

Industry	1970	1974	1978	1986	1990
Basic	1.2	1.2	1.1	0.7	0.9
Chemicals	4.7	3.7	4.6	6.7	6.8
Engineering	2.5	2.7	2.6	4.5	5.1
Metal products	1.4	1.7	1.6	2.4	2.4
Machinery	2.5	1.9	2.4	2.7	2.6
Electronics	4.5	3.5	3.0	4.1	4.6
Transport	1.3	2.7	2.4	5.9	8.4
All industries	2.2	2.1	2.2	3.9	3.9

Source: IUI database

the period studied, rising from about 4 per cent in the early 1970s to almost 7 per cent in 1990. Of other industries, only transport was more research-intensive. Machinery and metal products had the relatively smallest expenditure on technology within engineering, R&D remaining at little above 2 per cent of turnover throughout the 1970s and 1980s.

Total R&D intensities in the private sector are shown in Table 35 for the EC, the United States and Japan. The figures are not really comparable with those reported for Swedish MNCs, since the former are based on the 50 biggest R&D spenders in each respective region (suggesting an overestimate relative to the figures for the Swedish MNCs). In the EC and Japan, the trends again resemble those reported for Swedish companies. The levels of R&D intensity rose substantially in the mid 1980s, after which the rate of increase stagnated. In this respect, companies in the United States display a different picture, as their R&D intensity rose constantly during the entire period.

Table 35 Total R&D intensity (total R&D/total turnover) of the 50 largest R&D spenders in different regions, selected years 1984–92, per cent

Region	1984	1988	1992
EC	2.7	4.4	4.5
United States	2.9	3.3	3.7
Japan	4.2	5.4	5.8

Source: EC Commission (1994)

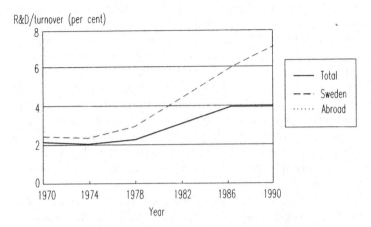

Figure 11 Total, domestic and overseas R&D intensity of Swedish
MNCs, selected years 1970–90, per cent
Source: Fors and Svensson (1994)

Dividing Swedish MNCs into a domestic and a foreign compon-
ent,[6] Figure 11 shows that the total R&D intensity represents the
weighted average of a very disparate level at home and abroad. The
intensities in the Swedish constituent parts and in the MNCs as a
whole amounted to some 7 per cent and 4 per cent respectively in
1990. Throughout, R&D intensity has been at a lower level in the
foreign units, where it increased slowly from only 0.7 per cent to
1.2 per cent between 1970 and 1990.[7] The expansion of foreign
manufacturing operations meant that the average R&D intensity
of the Swedish MNCs remained constant between 1986 and 1990,
although R&D intensity increased both in the foreign and in the
domestic operations.

It may be noted that foreign-owned affiliates in Sweden had an
R&D intensity amounting to 1.7 per cent and 3.0 per cent in 1986
and 1991 respectively (Statistics Sweden, 1993). Studies of aggregate operations by foreign affiliates across industries in various
industrialized countries have generally observed a lower R&D
intensity, on average, by comparison with the host country. The
United States represents an exception, with foreign affiliates –
especially in pharmaceuticals and machinery – as research-
intensive as domestic firms (OECD, 1994a).

In the home operations of Swedish MNCs, R&D intensity
was roughly stable during the 1970s but rose steadily from 1978

onwards. In fact, the high growth in total R&D intensity of Swedish MNCs 1978–86 is wholly explained by the increase in the Swedish units.[8] As of 1986, R&D expenditures at home corresponded to 6 per cent of sales, which represented an approximate doubling compared with eight years earlier. In the late 1980s, however, both R&D expenditures and manufacturing output weakened at home. In some industries, such as engineering, turnover actually declined in real terms, while R&D expenditures remained constant or increased marginally. The chemical industry, especially pharmaceuticals, represents a marked exception, as the R&D intensity increased strongly parallel to a rapid growth in manufacturing output at home.

Let us again compare the technological 'input' indicator, R&D, with the possible 'output' indicator, 'number of patent applications', now in the case of the Swedish MNCs. Table 36 shows that between 1974 and 1990 the number of applications in Sweden fluctuated considerably within several industries, which partly depends on variation in which firms have been included. This is especially the case in basic industries, where some major MNCs in iron and steel were missing from the survey in 1978–86. The distribution of patent applications in 1990 across industries resembles the distribution of R&D expenditures, however, although chemicals had a relatively higher and basic industries a lower frequency of patent applications. This reflects differences in the orientation of R&D across industries, with chemicals having a

Table 36 Number of patent applications in Sweden by Swedish MNCs, by industry, 1974–90

Industry	1974	1978	1986	1990	Percentage distribution in 1990
Basic	66	82	9	18	4
Chemicals	46	66	110	154	29
Other	76	91	22	12	2
Engineering	316	396	451	344	65
Metal products	9	62	51	76	14
Machinery	84	81	112	90	17
Electronics	176	169	237	104	20
Transport	47	84	51	74	14
All industries	504	635	592	528	100

Source: Swedish Patent and Registration Office

86

particularly heavy emphasis on generic research. On the whole, the rank of industries in patent applications corresponds to their position in R&D intensity. The large increase in patent applications recorded in chemicals (not only pharmaceuticals) is consistent with the rapidly growing R&D intensity in that industry.

The number of patent applications is unevenly distributed across Swedish MNCs. About 10 firms accounted for 402 out of 528 applications in 1990. As many as 64 out of 119 MNCs did not apply for any patents in that year. This reflects the high concentration recorded for R&D expenditures in Swedish MNCs. Indeed, there turns out to be a close correlation between which firms have invested in R&D and which have applied for patents, verifying that R&D to some extent does show up in the form of patent applications.[9]

Of all applications for patents in Sweden, however, Swedish MNCs accounted for only 17 per cent in 1990, i.e. a much smaller share than R&D expenditures. In the United States, the top 50 MNCs accounted for 20 per cent of all domestic patent applications (UN, 1992).[10] In fact, the number of domestic patent applications sought by Swedish MNCs has grown slowly when compared to the development of R&D expenditures or R&D intensity, which corresponds with the trends observed in Table 32 on the national level.

How should these patterns in patent applications be interpreted? It appears that technical progress recorded by MNCs in particular is now showing up in other ways than through patents, although there are exceptions. Large firms are providing increasingly complex packages of products and services, where competitiveness is based on the entire concept rather than on individual bits of advanced technology. On the other hand, Swedish MNCs have been increasingly active in applying for patents abroad, as in the EU. The comparisons across industries and firms indicate that patent statistics remain of some use for studying the output of R&D, although far from the whole story is conveyed.

R&D IN FOREIGN AFFILIATES

The bulk of R&D undertaken by MNCs has so far remained located in their countries of origin. The location of R&D has consequently been much less internationalized than that of production. Economies of scale and difficulties in co-ordinating R&D

between geographically disparate locations, together with the connection between the specific assets of MNCs and the nature of home country institutions, provide the most obvious explanation. Again, this does not mean that technology creation has been inward-looking and isolationist. Impulses from abroad can in many cases be assimilated through the hiring of foreign personnel, personal visits to foreign countries, publications, seminars, etc., but tend to require a concentrated knowledge base.

Still, a degree of decentralization of R&D has been observed for decades in MNCs based in several countries. In MNCs from the United States, foreign R&D has mainly been motivated by the need to adjust to the preferences and requirements of local markets.[11] Ronstadt (1984) found that most R&D units abroad take the form of technical service labs which facilitate transfers of technology from the parent company to foreign units. In the case of Japanese-owned foreign affiliates, studies have similarly found an emphasis on adaptation to local conditions, but have also pointed to the upgrading of production processes as well as the aim to search for new technologies (OECD, 1994).

Recent work indicates that this picture is now less relevant than it used to be. The growing importance of product diversification, economies of scope, shorter product cycles and rapid obsolescence require closer interaction between the different stages of the value-added chain. This also includes favourable conditions for feedback from customers, with consequences for the localization of production as well as R&D (UN, 1992; UNCTAD, 1993). The possible gains of acquiring existing technology from competitors, including the recruitment of experts and qualified personnel where that is feasible, may also motivate a greater emphasis on foreign R&D for the purpose of technology sourcing.[12] Hence, a greater number of rivalling forces now influence the location of R&D.

Although some of the Swedish MNCs have placed entire 'R&D laboratories' outside Sweden, these remain small and few in number. Altogether, the R&D laboratories were reported as having only 388 employees altogether as of 1990. Most foreign R&D is, in fact, carried out by manufacturing affiliates in conjunction with production.[13]

Table 37 depicts how the ratios of foreign to total R&D have developed between 1970 and 1990. In aggregate manufacturing, the foreign share increased from less than 9 per cent to 14 per cent in the early 1970s. In the second half of the 1980s, the share of

Table 37 Share of R&D abroad for Swedish MNCs, by industry, 1970–90, per cent

Industry	1970	1974	1978	1986	1990
Basic	0.1	10.7	6.4	2.1	25.0
Chemicals	9.8	13.3	12.6	13.2	17.0
Engineering	9.8	15.2	14.6	12.8	18.2
Metal products	1.3	0.0	15.0	16.0	21.4
Machinery	13.8	34.6	37.3	45.1	55.6
Electronics	11.6	11.6	9.3	17.1	25.5
Transport	0.3	8.9	3.8	3.6	5.6
All industries	8.6	14.0	13.6	13.0	18.6

Source: IUI database

R&D undertaken abroad increased again, this time to almost 19 per cent. As a comparison, it may be noted that the share of foreign R&D in manufacturing United States MNCs increased from 6 per cent in 1970 to about 10 per cent in 1989. In the case of German MNCs, employment in R&D personnel abroad is reported to have grown more rapidly than total employment abroad (UN, 1992). MNCs based in Finland, which like Sweden is a small country, have strongly expanded their foreign share of R&D, which rose from 15 per cent in 1987 to 29 per cent in 1992. The substantial devaluation of the Finnish mark explains part of the increase, but far from all of it. Table 38 shows that the foreign share became particularly large in machinery and transport. Thus foreign R&D in general appears to display trends which resemble

Table 38 Share of R&D abroad for 20 large Finnish MNCs, by industry, 1987 and 1992, per cent

	Share of R&D abroad	
Industry	1987	1992
Food	6	26
Wood, paper and pulp	6	8
Chemicals	10	26
Metals and metal products	15	28
Machinery and transport	28	47
Electronics	11	26
Other	33	40
All industries	15	29

Source: Åkerblom (1993)

those experienced by Swedish MNCs, but with expansion taking place at a lower level in MNCs based in larger home countries.

Among industries, engineering and chemicals have had an almost identical proportion of R&D located abroad, which is close to that of the aggregate. In basic industries, there have been marked shifts over time, especially in the form of a steep rise during the late 1980s. This was mainly associated with the extensive R&D undertaken by acquired affiliates in pulp and paper. One should bear in mind the relatively low level of absolute R&D expenditure in basic industries, however, which allowed a modest rise in foreign R&D to generate a substantial increase relative to the home base.

Within engineering, foreign R&D has increased markedly in machinery and electronics. Throughout the reported period, machinery has experienced a higher level of R&D than other constituents of engineering. In 1970, 15 per cent of R&D in this industry was located abroad, growing to more than 50 per cent in 1990. In electronics, foreign affiliates accounted for 25 per cent of total R&D in the same year. All industries actually experienced some expansion of foreign R&D between 1986 and 1990. It should be noted that transport exhibited the smallest share of foreign R&D, as the parent companies were responsible for close to 95 per cent in 1990. Since transport has the greatest weight in total R&D, it is the continued emphasis on home country R&D in this industry which explains the modest internationalization in engineering as a whole. At the same time, transports is *de facto* marked by intensifying collaboration in product development across national borders. The stories of SAAB-General Motors and Volvo-Renault in the early 1990s send mixed signals concerning the extent to which this will also show up in formal equity relations.

To what extent have the characteristics and functions of foreign R&D changed during its recent expansion? In the 1970s, the major part of foreign R&D in Swedish MNCs was – as in the case of United States firms – directed towards the adaptation of products and processes developed at home for local use abroad. Studying Swedish affiliates in 1978, for example, Zejan (1990) found that their R&D intensity was related to the degree to which the parent company concentrated R&D on the development of new products.

Let us attempt some observations about the distribution of R&D at the level of the firm in recent years. For 1990, Figure 12

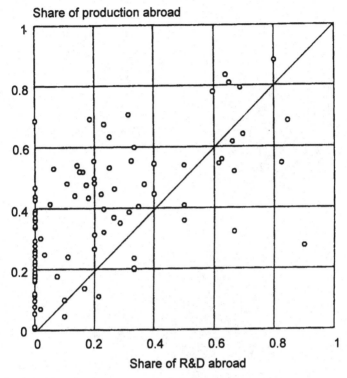

Figure 12 Overseas production and overseas R&D of Swedish MNCs, 1990. Number of observations, 96 MNCs. Only firms undertaking R&D are included, as the ratio of overseas to total R&D is not known for firms not undertaking R&D

Source: IUI database

displays a positive relationship between the proportions of R&D and of manufacturing undertaken abroad. Broadly speaking, firms which locate a relatively large share of manufacturing abroad continue to do the same in the case of R&D.[14] As discussed in the preceding chapter, those Swedish MNCs which are the most internationalized in terms of production tend to be horizontally rather than vertically integrated. Adjustment of products or production processes to foreign markets is in line with an emphasis on foreign R&D. This is highly applicable to machinery, in which 80 per cent of employment and 55 per cent of R&D in the Swedish MNCs were located abroad on average in 1990. Although most firms are more internationalized in respect of manufacturing than in respect

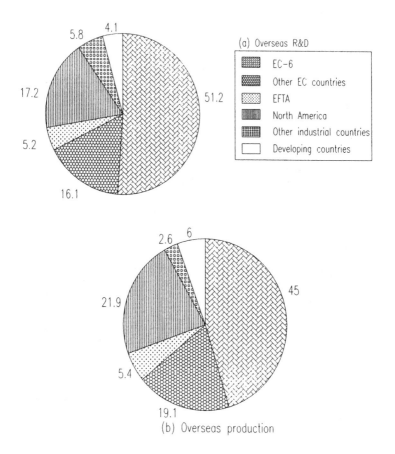

Figure 13 Distribution of Swedish MNCs' overseas R&D and overseas production, by region, 1990, per cent. (a) Overseas R&D. (b) Overseas production
Source: Fors and Svensson (1994)

of R&D, 16 are found below the diagonal line in Figure 12, meaning that a larger share of R&D than of manufacturing has been located abroad.[15]

The geographical distribution of Swedish MNCs' foreign production and R&D is reported in Figure 13 as of 1990. On the whole, the distribution of R&D appears to match that of production fairly well, especially in Europe, North America and EFTA. 'Other industrial countries' are overrepresented in terms of R&D, however. Meanwhile, affiliates in developing countries display a smaller share of foreign R&D than of manufacturing, but perhaps not as small as might have been expected, given their level of income.

Tables 39 and 40 report R&D expenditures and R&D intensities respectively in foreign manufacturing affiliates across countries/regions in chemicals, engineering and for all industries. Obviously, there is considerable variation in the localization of R&D, with a certain preference for the most advanced economies, which can be expected to offer favourable conditions. Some 'distant' markets are also characterized by high research intensity, although Japan is not.

In Table 41 foreign manufacturing affiliates are divided into two separate groups based on the way in which they were originally established. In line with previous chapters, own technology may be more effectively transferred to new ventures, while acquisition serves as a means of supplementing own assets with new ones.

Table 39 R&D expenditure of foreign manufacturing affiliates, by region, 1990, SEK million

	R&D expenditures		
Region	*Chemicals*	*Engineering*	*All industries*
Belgium	9	316	337
France	77	81	187
Italy	50	127	210
Netherlands	10	112	139
Germany	72	396	547
United Kingdom	2	198	243
Denmark	27	47	80
Other EC countries	0	107	122
Total EC	247	1,384	1,865
EFTA	9	118	143
North America	149	336	489
Japan	4	13	17
Other industrialized countries	4	139	143
Developing countries	1	113	114
All regions	414	2,103	2,771

Note: R&D expenditures in foreign manufacturing affiliates do not need to equal foreign R&D expenditures at the firm level; R&D expenditures at firm level also include R&D in 'R&D laboratories' and in sales affiliates. Furthermore, there are some missing values in the R&D variable at the affiliate level.
Source: IUI database

Table 40 R&D intensities among foreign manufacturing affiliates, by region, 1990, per cent

	R&D intensities		
Region	*Chemicals*	*Engineering*	*All industries*
Belgium	1.49	1.62	1.57
France	2.47	1.26	1.19
Italy	2.44	1.05	1.30
Netherlands	1.45	1.29	1.03
Germany	1.62	2.25	1.88
United Kingdom	1.48	1.48	1.19
Denmark	2.09	2.09	0.96
Other EC countries	1.35	1.57	1.24
Total EC	1.71	1.57	1.39
EFTA	0.27	4.30	1.38
North America	3.23	1.23	1.32
Japan	0.93	0.74	0.71
Other industrialized countries	0.92	2.50	2.29
Developing countries	0.04	0.78	0.64
All regions	1.60	1.50	1.33

Note: R&D intensities in foreign manufacturing affiliates do not need to correspond to foreign R&D intensities at the firm level; R&D intensities at firm level also include R&D in 'R&D laboratories' and in sales affiliates. Furthermore, there are some missing values in the R&D variable at the affiliate level.
Source: IUI database

Table 41 R&D expenditure of foreign manufacturing affiliates with different entry mode, by industry, 1978 and 1990; 1990 constant prices, SEK million

	1978			*1990*		
	Entry mode			*Entry mode*		
Industry	*Greenfield*	*Aquisition*	*All affiliates*	*Greenfield*	*Aquisition*	*All affiliates*
Basic	2	2	4	25	178	203
Chemicals	75	41	116	183	231	414
Engineering	364	279	643	872	1,231	2,103
Other	42	88	130	13	39	52
All industries	483	410	893	1,093	1,679	2,771

Note: See note on Table 39.
Source: IUI database

Table 42 R&D intensities among foreign manufacturing affiliates with different entry mode, by industry, 1978 and 1990, per cent

	1978			1990		
	Entry mode			Entry mode		
Industry	Greenfield	Aquisition	All affiliates	Greenfield	Aquisition	All affiliates
Basic	0.04	0.04	0.04	0.54	0.65	0.63
Chemicals	1.38	1.35	1.37	1.65	1.57	1.60
Engineering	0.82	1.31	0.98	1.11	2.01	1.50
Other	1.02	0.82	0.88	0.30	0.69	0.52
All industries	0.81	1.01	0.89	1.11	1.54	1.33

Note: See note on Table 40.
Source: IUI database

While most affiliates in 1978 had been established as new ventures, some two-thirds of those in existence in 1990 had been acquired. Table 42 shows that R&D intensity was somewhat higher for acquisitions in 1978, especially in engineering. The difference was magnified in 1990, when both engineering and other industries had about twice as high an R&D intensity in acquisitions as in greenfield operations. This indicates that acquisitions generally are more important in adapting products to local markets compared with greenfield operations, partly through sourcing of technology. In this respect the chemical industry forms an exception, with acquired companies having a marginally lower R&D intensity than new ventures on average, which is in line with a particularly great reliance on own technology in this industry.

Thus there are indications that the shift towards foreign R&D in recent years has been associated with a shift towards longer-term R&D more generally applicable abroad. One estimate holds that more than half of foreign R&D by Swedish MNCs in 1990 was directed towards the development of new products and processes (Norgren, 1993). There has also been increased integration of own R&D with existing knowledge creation in acquired firms, especially in basic industries. Still, the actual evidence suggests that the main purpose of locating R&D abroad so far remains associated with the adaptation of products and processes developed at headquarters.

We have seen that the share of R&D undertaken abroad was almost constant among Swedish MNCs from 1970 until the mid

1980s. There are several explanations for the increase which occurred in the latter half of the decade. In a general sense, the increasing complexity of products and processes, resulting in rising cost requirements in R&D, together with fierce competition, has spurred an internationalization of technology creation. At the same time, the high level of industrial R&D in Sweden together with the expansion of the public sector created excess demand for engineers and researchers. A regulated labour market, repressed wage differentials and a relatively low return from higher education have also restrained the supply of qualified personnel, especially engineers. Such factors are likely to have pushed a relocation of R&D, adding to more pull-oriented considerations.

It should also be noted that the 'technological system' in Sweden appears to have become polarized, or fragmented, with a stronghold of academia involved in pure research and individual innovators on the one hand and, on the other, large, streamlined firms which emphasize product development in fields where they are already well established. In between there has not been a sufficient supply of entrepreneurs able and willing to bridge the gap between ideas and their commercialization in new companies. While this is highly applicable to most parts of engineering, the pharmaceutical sector – with its great need of generic, long-term research – has continued to benefit from mutually enhancing knowledge creation in state-financed hospitals and universities and in the private sector.

R&D AND INTERNATIONAL COMPETITIVENESS

We know that spending resources on R&D may grant firms a technologically based competitive edge, thereby raising productivity, foreign market shares and profits. Furthermore, a number of empirical studies have shown that technological capabilities created through R&D play a major role in the emergence and further expansion of MNCs.[16] This should come as no surprise, since the very existence of MNCs hinges on the possession of firm-specific assets which cannot easily be traded at arm's length.

Less attention has been paid to the converse relationship, namely that operations in foreign markets may be a prerequisite for achieving the economies of scale and financial strength needed for R&D. An international network of operations may also increase the ability to gain from technical progress, since it tends to be difficult to trade technology in the market.[17] In other words, the rate of return on each R&D dollar spent may increase with the internationalization of firms. This should apply especially to firms based in small economies, and in cases where success in foreign markets requires a high technology content. Thus we can expect a two-way relationship: the creation and management of technology influence the existence and structures of MNCs, while the development of MNCs at the same time influences technical progress.

Examining the possibility of a mutual relationship between R&D and foreign sales on the basis of data from the United States, Hirschey (1981) found impact of foreign sales on R&D expenditures to be significant. In his specification, internationalization was not affected by R&D, however, which raises doubts concerning the interpretation of the results.

For the population of Swedish MNCs, Figure 14 demonstrates a clear-cut positive relationship between R&D intensity, measured as a firm's total R&D expenditures divided by total sales, and degree of internationality, measured as the ratio of foreign sales to total sales. Foreign sales are, in turn, measured as exports from the home country plus foreign production, as this should produce a better measure of international competitiveness than either exports or foreign production taken on their own. As can be seen, the lower right-hand corner is empty, meaning that firms which have a low ratio of foreign to total sales simply do not have high R&D intensity. The Pearson correlation coefficient between the two variables is 0.41, which is significant at the 1 per cent level.[18]

A closer examination of the reciprocal relationship between R&D expenditures and foreign sales allows of additional observations (Svensson and Fors, 1994). The analysis is based on the data provided by Swedish MNCs in the 1986 and 1990 surveys, which contain more detailed information on this relationship than previous questionnaires. Using a simultaneous regression method, a positive two-way relationship is verified between R&D intensity and the degree of internationalization at each point in time. R&D activity which aims at both product and process innovation helps explain success in MNCs' penetration of foreign markets. Sales are also found to be positively related to the

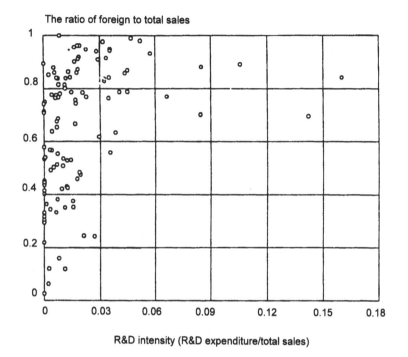

Figure 14 R&D intensity of Swedish MNCs and the ratio of foreign to total sales, 1990. Number of observations, 116 MNCs
Source: Svensson and Fors (1994)

presence of scale economies at the plant level, which provide incumbent firms with an advantage. An expansion of foreign sales is found to induce greater expenditure on product-related R&D, applying particularly to pharmaceuticals, telecommunications and automobiles.

It may also be noted that a high world market concentration in product markets shows up as associated with greater commitment to R&D at the firm level. While determining the actual link between market structure and technical progress is a complex matter which lies beyond the scope of this study, this observation is consistent with the notion that industries with oligopolistic elements are particularly marked by strategies other than pricing, such as advertising, product differentiation and R&D.

INTERNATIONAL TECHNOLOGY TRANSFERS

MNCs are probably of even greater importance for international technology transfers than for knowledge creation, as transaction costs typically make it expensive to export technology to 'outsiders'. Firms may transfer technology in a number of formal and informal ways: manuals and publications, imports of machinery, equipment and intermediate goods, patents, licences, and so forth. Licensing is often viewed as a major alternative to FDI, preferred when companies for some reason find it advantageous to trade technology rather than internalize it. At least as far as Swedish MNCs are concerned, however, it is obvious that most licensing and royalty payments occur within company groups. This follows the observation that more than 80 per cent of the registered payments for technology sales of United States firms were made by foreign affiliates in 1970–85 (Grosse, 1989). For technology embodied in capital goods, there is similarly evidence of the dominant role of intra-firm trade.

It is often assumed that technology takes the form of a public good within the organization of MNCs, and is spread costlessly to its different parts. According to mainstream views (cf. Mansfield and Romeo, 1980), R&D-created knowledge is applied to production throughout the firm. In the case of MNCs which undertake the bulk of their R&D in the home country, the postulated direction of transfers is from the parent to affiliates located abroad. In practice, complete transfers may be neither possible nor desirable even within the networks of an MNC (cf. Markusen, 1994).

The mechanisms through which technology is spread within MNCs are still inadequately understood. Davidson and McFetridge (1985) concluded that technology is more likely to be internalized the closer it is to the main line of business in the group of companies. Empirical studies have found a shorter time lag when technology is transferred within a firm than when it is transferred between separate companies (Behrman and Wallender, 1976; Mansfield and Romeo, 1980; McFetridge, 1987). At the same time, the characteristics of groups, affiliates and host countries influence what technology transfers occur even within firms. Some small-scale surveys, such as Teece's (1977), have investigated the costs of intra-firm transfers through interviews with firm executives. Still, there have been few attempts so far to explain what determines the extent of technology transfers within MNCs.

Studying the IUI data from 1965 to 1990, Fors (1993) addresses the degree to which knowledge generated through R&D activities in the parent company is transferred to manufacturing affiliates. The parent company's R&D is included as a factor of production in the affiliates' production function. In line with previous work, e.g. Ravenscraft and Scherer (1982), R&D expenditures are hypothesized to influence productivity with a time lag of about four years. It turns out that the R&D impact is strongly significant. While no direct effects are observed from R&D undertaken in affiliates themselves, either on their own productivity or on that of other companies in the group, there is a highly significant interactive effect between affiliate R&D and parent R&D. This strengthens the impression that R&D in affiliates mainly improves their competence to utilize the technology of the parent firm. At the same time, forward vertical integration, measured as imports of intermediate products from the parent company, has a positive effect on the presence of a technology transfer, confirming that technology is partly embodied in intrafirm deliveries.

In addition to the technology transfers within MNCs, spillovers occur in the form of externalities to outside actors. As discussed in Chapter 2, this may show up as changes in product and export composition, higher factor productivity, etc.[19] The instruments include turnover of trained personnel, collaboration with local R&D institutions, exchange with local upstream and downstream producers, effects on competition, etc. (UN, 1992).

The extent to which technology is transferred to foreign affiliates, as well as the extent to which spill-overs occur, is related to the interplay between MNCs and local firms. Spill-over effects are typically costly from the perspective of an MNC, as they may create more potent local competitors. With three-quarters of world technology trade occurring between OECD countries (Vickery, 1986), capabilities are still redistributed mainly within the developed world. According to Kokko (1992), the technology transfer from parent to affiliates is larger the higher the income level of the host country. This again relates to the prevalence of multiple equilibria in knowledge creation. The more adept local partners are, the more fastidious the consumers and the stronger the local competition, the greater the motivation for MNCs to transfer technology and the greater the potential for spill-overs. While less developed countries may have a great need to receive technology transfers, they may consequently have weak opportunities for doing so as well as a low capacity to absorb technology.

Since older technologies can generally be obtained through arm's-length transactions in the form of purchases of licences or patents, FDI is the most important for transferring new technology. The overseas R&D carried out by MNCs is interesting in this respect, since it typically serves to adapt products and processes to the conditions and demand requirements of the specific host country (see pp. 87–96). The resulting knowledge may consequently be relatively easy for domestic firms to absorb or copy. This is especially the case with firms which are vertically linked to MNCs, upstream or downstream, or which co-ordinate their R&D activities with foreign affiliates. Increasing competition in the local market may induce domestic firms, first, to copy technology used by the MNC in the affiliates; second, to use existing technology more efficiently, or, third, to search for new technologies.

Foreign affiliates account for a large and important share of all R&D in several developing countries. In Singapore and the Republic of Korea, for example, foreign affiliates in the 1970s were estimated to undertake some 15 per cent of total R&D. Still, not only are MNC operations in R&D-intensive industries underrepresented in the developing world, but there is also relatively little local R&D. In 1989, only 4 per cent of the total foreign R&D expenditures undertaken by United States MNCs was located in developing countries (UN, 1992). As shown in Figure 13, the corresponding share was about the same for Swedish MNCs in 1990. While Swedish MNCs had a small share of total manufacturing in developing countries, however, the operations located there were on average relatively less oriented towards low R&D intensity. This is in line with a relatively strong presence in developing countries by Swedish MNCs in knowledge-intensive industries, as well as with an emphasis on production for local markets as compared with off-shore production by United States affiliates. Thus, in this case, the smaller home country has fewer operations in developing countries and fewer options for an immediate expansion of exports, but the ventures which have come about may be at least as interesting with regard to technology transfers.

Transfers of technology raise important issues from the perspective of home countries as well. In the Swedish case, the expansion of MNCs' operations abroad has stimulated R&D efforts at home. Furthermore, while supply and distribution channels have become highly internationalized, many technological linkages within the home country have remained important. High-level executives have, for example, cited the existence of well qualified functions in other firms as a major reason why their headquarters and research activities have remained located in Sweden. At the same time, the competition for resources, particularly regarding trained engineers and researchers, has been a limiting factor. The situation has been aggravated by institutional constraints, partly associated with tax and wage structures, which have hindered effective responses on the supply side. So far, R&D expenditures are still much less dispersed internationally than advanced manufacturing operations, necessitating highly effective transfers of knowledge and information from the Swedish parent companies to foreign subsidiaries.

EXPENDITURES ON TRAINING

Technology paves the way for rationalization which makes jobs redundant, but it also opens opportunities for expansion and new activities. Successful technical progress is dependent on the upgrading of skills in the work force. While official educational institutions have to play their part in training and producing experts, MNCs also make major contributions in the build-up of human capital (Katz, 1987; Yoshihara, 1988).

For a number of reasons, incentive problems may prevent the upgrading of competence and adaptability among the work force. The possible reasons include the inability of students to borrow against future income (Loury, 1981) and externalities which allow others to reap some of the profits (Lucas, 1990; Rauch, 1991). Because pay-offs accrue to actors other than those who undertake the investment, too little tends to be spent. In particular, workers may leave the company and take their skills with them, disrupting both company processes and the diffusion of knowledge, restraining investment in skills in the first place. Concerning on-the-job training, Becker (1993) counter-argues that firms should not underinvest in employees, since workers should accept lower wages in return for training. As systematic data are generally not available for individual firms and employees, it is difficult to examine the validity of such propositions.

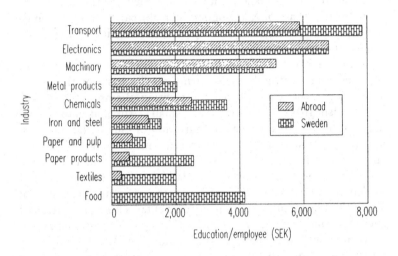

Figure 15 Expenditures on education and training per employee by Swedish MNCs, per industry, at home and abroad, 1990, SEK. The information is based on a relatively low response rate in the IUI questionnaire. Although 80 per cent of respondents answered the question a number of large MNCs are missing from the material
Source: IUI database

Let us consider the extent to which Swedish MNCs invest in their work force, at home and abroad, how such investment relates to R&D and whether any consequences of underinvestment can be observed. The expenditures on education and training (in SEK per employee) by Swedish MNCs in 1990 are shown in Figure 15 for domestic as well as foreign units across industries. There is a fairly strong resemblance to the pattern of R&D intensity, discussed above. Transport, electronics and machinery hold the leading positions, while chemicals are down in fifth place. Food also reports large expenditures at home, but nothing abroad. On the whole, however, R&D-intensive industries have the largest expenditures on education abroad per employee, followed by the capital-intensive industries of iron and steel, pulp and paper. Firms which exploit knowledge generated by their own R&D appear motivated to invest more in their personnel. Furthermore, industries with a high R&D intensity report about as high an intensity of training expenditures abroad as at home. In machinery, which has an extremely large share of R&D undertaken abroad, training expenditures per employee are even reported to be higher in foreign operations than in the home country.

As in the case of R&D, one might anticipate differences in training expenditures between firms on the basis of their size. Table 43 presents the reported composition of employees in 1989 in Swedish firms categorized as 'small', 'subcontractors' and 'large'.[20] Small firms have a concentration of blue-collar workers, which are the least represented in large firms. Large firms have an overrepresentation of specialists and white-collar workers, while subcontractors employ a relatively large number of unskilled workers. As with large firms, the estimates presented in Table 44 indicate that global operations entail a high proportion of specialists and white-collar workers. Thus the internationalization of companies both requires skills and provides the resources which are needed to finance and exploit them. As discussed by Braunerhjelm (1991), Swedish subcontractors tend to have low R&D intensity and cover simple operations. Many continue to have great difficulty in coping with the internationalization of Swedish MNCs and competition from foreign subcontractors. Yet their demand for skilled workers remains low.

Table 45 classifies firms according to expenditure on training per employee in 1990. The second column shows the presence of a connection with R&D, which is particularly evident for the category which invests the most in human capital.[21] There is also a

Table 43 Distribution of employment in Swedish manufacturing: small firms, subcontractors and large firms, 1989, per cent

Category of employee	Small	Subcontractors	Large
Executive staff	5	3	2
Specialist[a]	9	7	11
White-collar[b]	16	15	29
Blue-collar[b]	46	35	25
Unskilled	24	40	33
Total	100	100	100

a Includes middle management.
b White-collar and blue-collar workers have formal education corresponding to university and upper secondary school, respectively.
Source: Braunerhjelm (1991)

Table 44 Employment categories for the global operations of Swedish manufacturing MNCs, 1988, per cent and SEK thousand

Category of employee	Percentage of total employees	Percentage of total labour costs	Labour costs per employee (SEK thousand)
Executive staff	3	5	357
Specialist[a]	7	12	290
White-collar[b]	31	31	181
Blue-collar[b]	25	26	186
Unskilled	34	26	136
Total	100	100	179[c]

a Includes middle management.
b White-collar and blue-collar workers have formal education corresponding to university and upper secondary school, respectively
c This is a weighted average.
Source: Calculations at IUI

Table 45 Swedish manufacturing MNCs classified according to level of expenditure on training, 1990, average of each category

Training/ employee (SEK)	R&D/ employee (SEK thousand)	Average turnover (SEK million)	Yearly salary (SEK thousand)			Value added/ employee (SEK thousand)		
			Home	EC	Total abroad	Home	EC	Total abroad
0	6	142	209	145	143	283	210	218
1–1,000	20	1,504	243	201	198	409	280	277
1,001–2,000	9	1,525	231	212	203	343	305	291
over 2,000	80	3,912	230	226	220	292	375	348

Note: Foreign operations include only manufacturing affiliates.
Source: IUI database

positive correlation with firm size. Bearing in mind the difficulty of comparing absolute values across countries owing to variation in, e.g., exchange rates and real prices, some interesting observations can still be made with regard to the pattern of wages and value added per worker at home and abroad for different companies.

It may be noted that firms without any expenditures on training record higher average labour productivity as well as wage levels at home than abroad. These firms are generally small and have limited foreign operations. As expenditures on training rise, there is no clear-cut connection with the level of labour productivity or wages in the home country, as can further be seen from Table 45. In foreign manufacturing on the whole, as well as in the EC, wages and labour productivity are both unequivocally higher in firms with relatively large expenditures on training. However, value added per worker increases much faster than wages, accounting for increasing profits. Those MNCs which report the greatest training expenditures per employee had considerably higher value added per worker abroad, especially in the EC, than they had at home. The wage level was still higher in Sweden than abroad. As we have seen, this situation has arisen after a period of rapid progress in manufacturing abroad and declining operations at home by the knowledge-intensive Swedish MNCs.

According to these observations, investment in worker skills by Swedish MNCs was associated with a greater rise in productivity than in wages, possibly supporting the stance that too little may be spent on training. At the same time, a discrepancy between productivity and wages, which increases in training expenditures, has only been observable in foreign operations. This may help to explain why so much was invested in the training of foreign personnel in the first place. Together with the fact that resources are expended on training in foreign units to a relatively large extent, as compared with R&D, this also suggests that there is a particularly large potential for spill-over effects on host economies from investment in human capital. Conclusive evidence in this respect requires more detailed analysis at the firm level, however. As data on training expenditures are lacking for a number of large Swedish MNCs, it is also important to expand the data set in this respect. Finally, the picture conveyed here may well have been specific to Swedish MNCs at the end of the 1980s.

6

EUROPEAN INTEGRATION AND RESTRUCTURING BY MULTINATIONALS

INTRODUCTION

From previous chapters it is clear that the late 1980s witnessed drastic changes in the organizational structure of Swedish MNCs, with implications for employment, trade, and technology creation, for example. The developments were closely associated with a changing relationship between the parent companies and their manufacturing affiliates in the EC, which attained a greatly expanded role in respect of overall production, trade and R&D within the corporate groups.

Those moves by Swedish MNCs were not an isolated phenomenon. At the time, there was also a marked expansion of FDI into the EC from the other EFTA countries, North America and Japan, as well as much larger flows between the member countries of the EC. Obviously, there was a connection with the launching of the Single Market programme, first announced in 1985.

In spite of decades of gradual economic integration, the relatively small European countries had remained notably heterogeneous up to this time, with exchange between them hampered by a host of technical and administrative barriers. The expectation of a single market with uniform playing rules in goods as well as factor markets throughout the EC brought about a completely new situation. The member countries were to revise their entire legislative framework, abolishing a range of regulations which accounted for national safe havens. The expected changes concerned all firms in the market, whether based within the EC or not.

Various reactions were triggered in policy-making around the world, including North America, the increasingly lagging planned economies of Eastern and Central Europe and the developing world. In several places, there was an intensified pursuit of liberalization on a regional basis. There were also other impulses towards reform and restructuring, contributing in one way or another to the overhaul of the old order on the far side of the Berlin wall. For industry outside the EC, however, the strongest responses were recorded among the small, highly developed EFTA countries. This, in turn, would have implications for the integration process itself.

Although there have been many studies of responses in FDI to the establishment of the Single Market, the lack of data still accounts for limited information about the restructuring of MNCs' operations themselves, and about the consequences for individual countries. Thus, building on the findings of the previous chapters, we here survey the connections between regional integration in the EC, the restructuring of Swedish MNCs and the resulting impacts, particularly from the home country perspective. The chapter starts out with a brief discussion of the stages in regional liberalization. This is followed by an examination of the pattern of FDI in the late 1980s, with special attention to the differences between the EC and EFTA countries. In order to analyse the effects of the changed pattern of FDI, the restructuring by Swedish MNCs is then studied in greater detail. Finally, we consider implications from the home country perspective.

EUROPEAN INTEGRATION AND THE SINGLE MARKET

Regional integration takes many shapes but, to simplify, four main stages can be distinguished. The most commonly adopted are *free trade areas* and *customs unions*. In free trade areas, tariffs are abolished between the member countries, but policies toward the rest of the world are left uncoordinated. In a customs union, the participating nations also adopt a common external trade policy. The third category is *common markets*, which aim at facilitating free flows not only of goods but also of services, and production factors such as capital and labour (the 'four freedoms'). To achieve this, national rules and standards must be harmonized and liberalized among the member states. Finally, an *economic union* can be regarded as the most far-reaching regional arrangement, wherein both monetary and fiscal policies are co-ordinated at a supranational level.

Europe has provided examples of several different integration schemes. The European Free Trade Association (EFTA) established in 1960, partly as a response to the formation of the European Economic Community (EEC, later the EC) three years earlier, has constituted a free trade area with no external policy co-ordination. The EEC encompassed a customs union of France, West Germany, Italy and the Benelux countries. In 1973, the UK, Ireland and Denmark left EFTA to join the EC, and a free trade agreement covering most manufactured products was signed between the EC and each EFTA country. EC enlargement continued in the 1980s with Greece joining in 1981, and Spain and Portugal in 1986.

The poor economic record which had plagued the EC since the oil crises of the 1970s called for new solutions. The new competition emerging from Asia and slow technological progress in Europe, as compared with the United States and Japan, accentuated the need for revival. Parts of the problem were blamed on the limited *de facto* integration between the member states. Although free trade within the EC was supposed to have been accomplished through the customs union, there were many exceptions. Instead of tariffs, differing technical, hygiene and other standards, as well as national quotas on imports of many products, severely impeded the free movement of goods. Services, capital flows and the mobility of workers were subject to even more constraints. In many industries, European firms were too small to exploit economies of scale, but too large for their national domestic markets, resulting in insufficient competition and monopolistic pricing (Cecchini, 1988).

Thus, in 1985, the European Commission announced plans for establishing the Single Market by the year 1993. The proposal was reinforced in 1987 with the passing of the Single European Act, which amounted to a binding commitment by the member states to complete the internal market. The immediate purpose was to fulfil the goal stipulated in the Treaty of Rome, i.e., to go beyond a customs union and create a common market, encompassing the 'four freedoms'. In short, the creation of the Single Market necessitated the removal of all interior barriers to trade, the opening up of public procurement and deregulation of factor markets. In addition, competition law was to be strengthened and more funds were to be provided in support of European R&D projects.

The restructuring of private industry was identified as the key force leading to social gains from the integration process.

Simulation models predicted lower prices and increased production, particularly in industries characterized by imperfect competition and scale economies (Cecchini, 1988; Smith and Venables, 1988). Incorporating dynamic effects through, e.g., enhanced capital accumulation and intensification of innovatory activity, led to prospects of even greater gains (Baldwin, 1989; Geroski, 1988).

The primary intention of the Single Market programme was to make it easier for EC-based companies to compete in other EC markets, and to facilitate specialization and rationalization of operations within the EC.[1] Regarding the rest of the world, it had merely been stated that internal liberalization would not occur at the expense of external relations, although other views were expressed occasionally. Whatever the circumstances, the Single Market programme fundamentally changed the conditions for doing business in Europe, its effects being felt not only by firms based within the EC.

Non-EC firms also foresaw the benefits of selling to one unified market rather than twelve heterogeneous ones. Even without an increase in external trade barriers, improved conditions within the Single Market provided an incentive for non-EC companies to expand production in the EC. Lower production costs for firms inside, relative to those outside, threatened the position of the latter in the EC market (Baldwin et al., 1994). In addition, expectations of higher market growth provided a further incentive to invest in the Community.[2]

FDI IN EUROPE: EC V. NON-EC COUNTRIES

As can be seen from Table 46, global FDI shifted in the late 1980s from the United States, the dominant recipient country in the first half of the decade, towards the EC. A considerable proportion – some 40 per cent of the total – consisted of intra-Community investment, in the form of cross-border mergers and alliances, while most of the rest originated in the United States, Japan and EFTA (UN, 1991).

The cross-border flows of investment, set in motion partly by the Single Market programme, exerted the strongest impact on the small and highly trade-dependent EFTA countries which bordered on the Community but were not themselves part of it. At that particular point in time, these countries experienced major changes in the magnitude of outward rather than inward FDI. In

Table 46   Inward cumulative flows of FDI in the OECD, 1971–80, 1981–6 and 1987–90, US$ million and per cent

Recipient	1971–80		1981–6		1987–90	
	US$ million	Percent	US$ million	Percent	US$ million	Percent
European Community	107,918	57	81,645	35	245,821	46
United States	56,276	30	129,405	55	225,307	42
EFTA	5,802	3	9,647	4	19,333	4
Rest of OECD	18,253	10	12,523	5	46,107	9
Total*	188,249	100	233,220	100	536,568	100

Source: OECD (1993a)
Note: EC includes the twelve member countries as of 1990.
*Percentages may not add up to 100 due to rounding off.

the late 1980s, they became the prime source of non-EC investment into the Community.

The development of net FDI (inflows minus outflows) in the EFTA countries from 1981 to 1992 is presented in Figure 16a. While the gap between outward and inward FDI widened modestly for EFTA as a whole in the first half of the 1980s, a major deficit evolved after 1987. Between 1988 and 1990, the yearly net outflow equalled US$17 billion, compared with close to zero in the early 1980s. In these years, substantial net outflows were recorded primarily for Sweden, but also for Switzerland and Finland. In Austria and Norway, on the other hand, outflows and inflows were of about the same magnitude.[3]

In the following years, most EFTA countries applied for membership of the Community and the European Economic Area (EEA) was formed.[4] The Swiss, however, did not vote in favour of the EEA, which led to the exclusion of Switzerland from membership negotiations with the EC. While the international recession led to a general slowdown in investment activity, it is still interesting to note that during 1991 and 1992 the investment balance evened out in all the major EFTA countries except Switzerland.

In Figures 16b and 16c, the corresponding developments in investment flows are depicted for the EC economies. Primarily as an effect of large British, German and, to some extent, French outward FDI, the EC deficit increased during 1986 and 1987. Net outflows from Germany and France continued to rise after 1987,

111

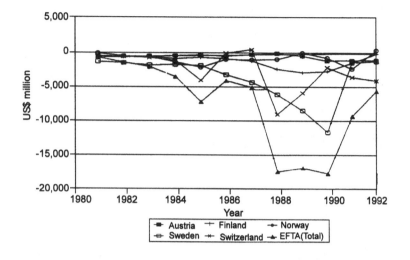

Figure 16(a) Net flows of FDI in EFTA countries, 1981–92, current
prices, US$ million
Sources: OECD (1993a), UNCTAD (1994)

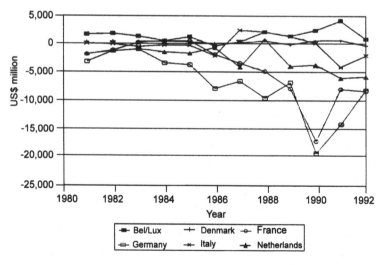

Figure 16(b) Net flows of FDI in selected EC countries, 1981–92,
current prices, US$ million
Sources: OECD (1993a), UNCTAD (1994)

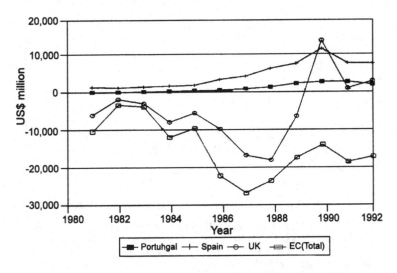

Figure 16(c)   Net flows of FDI in Portugal, Spain, the United Kingdom
and the EC as a whole, 1981–92, current prices, US$ million
Sources: OECD (1993a), UNCTAD (1994)

while Belgium, the UK, as well as the newcomers Spain and Portugal, experienced a growing surplus. For the EC as a whole, net outflows decreased between 1987 and 1990.

Figure 17 relates changes in FDI between the first and second half of the 1980s to the size of the respective economy (outflows/GDP are measured on the *x* axis, and inflows/GDP on the *y* axis). Among the EFTA countries, Sweden and Finland experienced much enhanced outflows while the ratio of inward FDI to GDP remained fairly stable. In Switzerland and Norway, both outward and inward FDI grew. Concerning the EC, Spain and Portugal received much larger inflows. The UK, the Netherlands and Belgium shifted to a situation of greater inflows as well as outflows, as is indicated by their north-easterly movement in the figure. France, finally, represents a special case, as its development resembles that of Sweden and Finland. In general, relatively small economies experienced the greatest shifts, and inflows of FDI increased mainly in those countries which were already located in the upper part of Figure 17 in the first half of the 1980s.

Consequently, the stock of inward FDI in Europe tilted in favour of the EC (Table 47). While the shares of EFTA and the EC

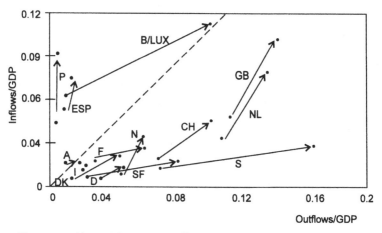

Figure 17 Changes in average inflows and outflows of FDI in EC and EFTA countries between the periods 1981–5 and 1986–90, relative to GDP in 1985 and 1990, respectively
Source: OECD (1993a, b)

were roughly stable in the first half of the decade, the EC's share of the total increased from 1985 to 1992. Spain accounted for by far the largest advance, while Belgium and Portugal also strengthened their relative positions as recipients of FDI. All EFTA countries reported declining shares in the same period. In 1990, small economies in the EC mostly reported a disproportionately large share of FDI relative to GDP, whereas the reverse applied to EFTA.

The extent to which the EC has been preferred as a location for FDI in Europe varies with the origin of the investment. Non-European firms have been especially reluctant to invest in non-EC countries in Europe. By the end of the 1980s, Canada, Japan and Australia all reported EC shares of more than 93 per cent of their total stocks of FDI in Europe (Table 48). By way of comparison, the EC accounted for only 86 per cent of GDP in OECD Europe.[5] The concentration of activity in the EC is most accentuated in respect of manufacturing. The relatively low share of 85 per cent reported for the United States in Table 48 is due to large American investments in Swiss wholesale and finance (US Department of Commerce). As can be seen in Table 49, the EC's share of United States FDI in European manufacturing was as high as 97 per cent in 1990. An equally large proportion of the accumulated flow of Japanese FDI 1951–89 to European manufacturing was found in the EC (Japan Ministry of Finance, 1991). The degree of

Table 47 Geographical distribution of inward stock of FDI in Western Europe, selected years 1980–92, and GDP in 1990, per cent

Country	1980	1985	1990	1992	Share of GDP in 1990
EC-12	90.0	89.8	91.2	91.6	87.6
Belgium/Luxembourg	3.7	3.7	4.9	6.8	2.9
Denmark	2.1	1.5	1.2	1.4	1.9
France	11.6	14.2	11.6	14.2	17.3
Germany	18.8	15.7	16.1	15.5	21.7
Greece	2.3	3.5	1.9	1.9	1.0
Ireland	1.9	2.0	0.7	0.6	0.6
Italy	4.6	8.0	7.8	7.5	15.9
Netherlands	9.8	10.6	9.8	10.0	4.1
Portugal	0.2	0.3	0.9	1.3	1.0
Spain	2.6	3.8	8.9	11.7	7.1
United Kingdom	32.3	26.5	27.4	20.7	14.1
EFTA	9.9	10.1	8.9	8.4	12.4
Austria	1.6	1.5	1.3	1.4	2.3
Finland	0.6	0.6	0.7	0.4	2.0
Norway	1.6	1.7	1.1	1.0	1.5
Sweden	1.7	2.0	1.6	1.7	3.3
Switzerland	4.4	4.3	4.2	3.9	3.3
Total Western Europe	100.0	100.0	100.0	100.0	100.0
Total in US$ billion	195.2	235.9	744.5	838.3	6,887.6

Source: UNCTAD (1994) and OECD (1993b)

concentration was even greater in employment terms. In 1989, the EC countries accounted for almost 99 per cent of the total work force in Japanese manufacturing affiliates in Europe (Table 50).

The development of inward FDI to Sweden strengthens the impression that non-EC countries have steadily become less attractive to non-European investors. While the United States was the largest single source country of FDI in Sweden in the 1960s and 1970s, American investment was virtually non-existent in the 1980s. Moreover, like other EFTA countries, Sweden was able to attract practically no Japanese FDI in manufacturing during the 1980s.

Taken together, flow as well as stock data of FDI suggest that the Single Market programme led to an investment diversion effect in the late 1980s, favouring EC countries at the expense of neighbouring EFTA. The case is further supported by analyses of gross

Table 48 EC share of the OECD countries' stock of FDI in Europe, 1990, per cent

Country	EC's share of each country's outward stock of FDI in Europe	Economic bloc
Finland[a]	58	EFTA
Austria[b]	75	EFTA
Sweden	76	EFTA
Norway	79	EFTA
Italy[a]	80	EC
Germany	83	EC
Netherlands[a]	84	EC
Belgium/Luxembourg[b]	85	EC
Denmark	85	EC
United States	85	Non-Europe
Spain	87	EC
Switzerland[a]	87	EFTA
France[a]	88	EC
United Kingdom[a]	88	EC
Canada[a]	93	Non-Europe
Japan	94	Non-Europe
Portugal[b]	100	EC
Australia[c]	100	Non-Europe

Note: a 1989, *b* 1988, *c* 1991.
Source: UN (1993a)

Table 49 Geographical distribution of the United States stock of FDI in Western Europe, 1972–90, per cent

Year	All sectors		Manufacturing	
	European Community	Other Western Europe	European Community	Other Western Europe
1972	81.1	18.9	89.1	10.9
1977	78.6	21.4	89.8	10.2
1982	77.1	22.9	90.2	9.8
1985	77.1	22.9	92.3	7.7
1990	84.8	15.2	96.8	3.2

Note: EC = Belgium, West Germany, France, Italy, Luxembourg, Netherlands, Denmark, Ireland, United Kingdom; for 1982 and 1985 above plus Greece; for 1990 above plus Spain and Portugal.
Source: US Department of Commerce (various years)

fixed investment flows in Europe during the late 1980s (Baldwin *et al.*, 1994). The effect appears to have been especially strong in manufacturing.

Table 50 Employment in Japanese-owned manufacturing firms in Europe, 1989

Country	Number of employees
United Kingdom	32,612
Spain	23,850
France	18,923
Germany	16,444
Belgium	6,250
Italy	5,400
Portugal	4,920
Ireland	2,910
Netherlands	2,800
Greece	1,128
Austria	750
Luxembourg	415
Sweden	366
Switzerland	320
Norway	70
Denmark	70
Finland	20
Total	117,268
Share in EC countries (per cent)	98.7

Source: Thomsen and Nicolaides (1991)

For a number of reasons, which are partly found in Chapter 3, Sweden experienced the most drastic changes in FDI. To recapitulate, the presence of relatively large MNCs increases the potential for outward FDI and implies high mobility on the part of Swedish industry. Second, compared with Norway and Finland, the Swedish economy is less dependent on primary industries and production that relies heavily on natural resources. In Norway, for instance, fishing and petroleum are the most important industries, neither of which was much affected by the Single Market programme (although fisheries have been a key issue in the debate over whether Norway should join the EC). Third, in the late 1980s, Swedish restrictions on capital movements were abolished. Fourth, the relative competitiveness of Sweden *vis-à-vis* the EC was affected by worsening conditions in the domestic economy, which was characterized by a shortage of labour together with high inflation and rising interest rates. As a consequence, real domestic investment was crowded out and there were generally unfavourable conditions for industrial expansion in the home country.

THE RESPONSE OF SWEDISH MNCS

How did the regional integration process affect the organization of Swedish MNCs? FDI statistics alone do not provide sufficient information for answering such questions. Let us look more closely at the restructuring which occurred in the late 1980s.

As shown in Table 51, there was a net addition of 79 manufacturing affiliates in the EC between 1986 and 1990. Among the EC countries, the number of affiliates declined only in France, while the total number in the EFTA countries fell from 96 to 89 – mainly owing to reductions in Finland and Switzerland. Developments in employment can be seen from Table 52. Between 1986 and 1990,

Table 51 Number of European manufacturing affiliates of Swedish MNCs, 1986 and 1990, by country

Country	Number of manufacturing affiliates in 1986	Number of manufacturing affiliates in 1990	Change between 1986 and 1990	Number of new entries
EC-12	334	413	+79	168
Belgium/ Luxembourg	13	17	+4	6
Denmark	40	46	+6	21
France	58	53	−5	15
Germany	76	90	+14	37
Ireland	5	6	+1	3
Italy	32	46	+14	16
Netherlands	25	35	+10	13
Portugal	9	10	+1	7
Spain[a]	21	23	+2	10
United Kingdom	55	87	+32	40
EFTA	96	89	−7	39
Austria	13	13	0	5
Finland	41	32	−9	14
Norway	28	34	+6	20
Switzerland	14	10	−4	0
Total Western Europe	430	502	+72	207

a Greece is included in the figure for Spain. Owing to insufficient observations the two countries cannot be presented separately.
Source: IUI database

Table 52 Distribution of employees in the parent companies and European manufacturing and sales affiliates of Swedish MNCs, 1986 and 1990, by country

Country	Number of employees in 1986	Number of employees in 1990	Change between 1986 and 1990 (per cent)
EC-12	166,580	213,678	+28
Belgium/ Luxembourg	11,129	15,361	+38
Denmark	15,025	14,508	−3
France	22,921	21,162	−8
Germany	34,096	49,155	+44
Ireland	1,212	1,563	+29
Italy	35,288	36,193	+3
Netherlands	10,703	14,466	+35
Portugal	4,010	4,363	+9
Spain[a]	9,603	14,955	+56
United Kingdom	22,593	41,952	+86
EFTA	29,922	24,287	−19
Austria	3,996	6,457	+62
Finland	11,779	6,713	−43
Norway	10,152	7,593	−25
Switzerland	3,995	3,524	−12
Sweden	375,000	306,387	−18
Total Western Europe	571,502	544,352	−5

a Greece is included in Spain. Due to too few observations, the two countries cannot be presented separately.
Source: IUI database

the number of employees in manufacturing and sales affiliates rose in all EC countries except France and Denmark, and by 28 per cent in the EC as a whole. The work force in EFTA subsidiaries, in contrast, declined by one-fifth,[6] and in the Swedish parent companies there was contraction to the extent of some 70,000 employees – a reduction of 18 per cent.

With the removal of internal trade restrictions, there was a reduced need to undertake production in each national market and a fall in the relative cost of serving an EC market from another EC location rather than from Sweden. Liberalization also favoured the exploitation of economies of scale in certain locations and the agglomeration of production characterized by knowledge spill-overs. The potential for relocation was greatest in activities whose competitiveness hinges on internationally mobile, firm-specific assets. For firms relying on access to Swedish raw materials, moving production was less of an option.

As shown in Table 53, except for the mixed category of 'other industries', Swedish MNCs increased the number of their production units in the EC in all industries. In EFTA, by contrast, the number of manufacturing affiliates grew only in basic industries. Table 54 translates these changes into output figures. Again, strong overall growth occurred throughout the EC except for the peripheral countries of Ireland and Portugal. Affiliates in EFTA recorded modest overall growth, except in the case of Austria, where MNCs in basic industries substantially increased their presence. The discrepancy between the three Nordic host countries is worth noting; whereas output grew by more than 60 per cent in Denmark it contracted in Finland and Norway. The decline in the latter two countries was entirely due to the trend in

Table 53 Number of European manufacturing affiliates of Swedish MNCs, 1986 and 1990, by industry and region

Industry	Number of manufacturing affiliates in 1986	Number of manufacturing affiliates in 1990	Change between 1986 and 1990
EC-12			
Basic	36	64	+28
Chemicals	44	62	+18
Engineering	200	239	+39
Other industries	54	48	−6
All industries	334	413	+79
EFTA			
Basic	7	10	+3
Chemicals	18	15	−3
Engineering	49	43	−6
Other industries	22	21	−1
All industries	96	89	−7
Total	430	502	+72

Source: IUI database

Table 54 Output from foreign manufacturing affiliates of Swedish MNCs in the EC and in EFTA countries, by industry, 1986 and 1990, current prices, SEK million

Country	All industries		Basic industries		Chemicals		Engineering	
	1986	1990	1986	1990	1986	1990	1986	1990
Belgium	10,465	15,966	778	1,586	137	569	9,263	13,486
France	12,540	17,784	1,457	4,902	1,203	2,880	8,300	8,502
Italy	16,779	26,653	0	2,529	634	1,995	16,033	22,130
Netherlands	6,030	12,625	1,514	5,113	703	685	3,296	5,890
Germany	18,797	47,157	3,292	23,117	1,991	3,790	10,876	19,248
Denmark	6,636	10,804	445	3,001	467	1,489	4,367	4,818
UK	8,764	27,332	1,087	8,034	420	1,258	6,056	14,954
Ireland	541	723	21	373	0	208	287	142
Spain	3,386	10,660	0	0	201	498	2,986	10,109
Portugal	1,007	1,383	771	1,094	0	2	30	18
Norway	4,413	4,071	794	1,220	933	1,239	1,910	1,044
Finland	3,906	3,772	470	770	556	1,410	2,213	1,007
Switzerland	1,384	1,819	116	130	96	135	1,136	1,554
Austria	1,512	4,958	183	3,071	401	411	788	1,476

Note: Output from affiliates is here defined as total sales less internal deliveries from the parent company.
Source: IUI database

engineering, where affiliate output dropped by more than 50 per cent. MNCs in engineering expanded primarily in Belgium, Germany, Italy, the Netherlands, Spain and the UK.

Swedish FDI in Europe has obviously been motivated by different aims in EC and EFTA countries. Table 55 shows that in the relatively small economies of Belgium, the Netherlands, Ireland and Portugal, exports amounted to more than 50 per cent of affiliate sales in 1990. The large Belgian and Dutch imports of intermediates from the parent company testify to vertical links with the home country. Owing to low labour costs, Portugal has attracted export-oriented ventures in textiles and clothing as well as some manufacturing in basic industries. A significant proportion of Portuguese affiliates' output is also sold in Sweden. Similar observations apply to Ireland.

With few exceptions, Swedish FDI in EFTA appears to have been motivated by access to local markets. Export intensities were low, especially considering the small size of the host economies, throughout EFTA, with the exception of Austria.[7] Despite the central position of Switzerland, Swiss affiliates exported less than a quarter of their output in 1990. Affiliates in Norway and Finland

Table 55 Propensity of Swedish-owned European affiliates to export and to import intermediate products from the parent company, by country, 1990, per cent

Country	Total exports/ sales	Exports to Sweden/ sales	Exports to third countries/ sales	Imports of intermediates from parent/sales
Large EC countries				
France	23	2	21	5
Germany	41	2	39	4
Italy	37	3	34	3
Spain	11	2	9	11
United Kingdom	13	1	12	11
Small EC countries				
Belgium	91	38	53	28
Denmark	39	9	30	2
Ireland	56	22	34	0
Netherlands	50	2	48	19
Portugal	79	11	68	3
EFTA countries				
Austria	60	1	59	1
Finland	17	9	8	4
Norway	23	16	7	3
Switzerland	24	3	21	4

Source: IUI database

exported an even smaller share of their sales to third countries than did those in Spain or the UK. By comparison, in the third Nordic country, Denmark, the corresponding figure was four times greater. These observations, together with the low dependence on parent supplies of intermediate products, point towards a greater emphasis on horizontal integration in the EFTA countries.

Differences in internal corporate structures may explain the noted concentration of Japanese and United States FDI in the EC. Several studies have shown that Japanese MNCs tend to specialize operations in the EC and then export about half the affiliates' output (cf. Kume and Totsuka, 1991; Thomsen and Nicolaides, 1991; Yamawaki, 1991).[8] According to the UN (1993b), American subsidiaries in the EC similarly operate in complex networks with vertical links between each other. The inability of EFTA in the late 1980s to attract manufacturing FDI from these countries reflects the fact that export-oriented operations in Europe generally gravitated towards the EC.

Summing up, like MNCs from other countries, not only did Swedish MNCs restructure their operations away from EFTA and towards the EC, as is seen from declining employment and output in EFTA and the converse in the EC, but their investments differed in character as between the two group of countries. Analyses of trade patterns show a high degree of specialization in the EC, whereas market-oriented purposes dominated in EFTA. Furthermore, the expansion by Swedish MNCs in the EC involved virtually all sectors, while it was mainly basic industries that were targeted in EFTA.

CONNECTIONS BETWEEN PARENTS AND AFFILIATES

The developments of the 1980s led to more far-reaching specialization of production within the Swedish MNCs, profoundly affecting the position of parents and affiliates. As home countries of MNCs have traditionally been relatively well endowed with capital, international specialization has normally resulted in the concentration of capital- and research-intensive activities at the parent company, while foreign affiliates have performed less advanced assembly operations or highly labour-intensive tasks. As we have seen, however, the foreign expansion of Swedish MNCs was not motivated primarily by cheap labour considerations. Expansion occurred in other high-income countries with sophisticated infrastructure, subcontractors and labour. Hence, these countries represent alternative locations for export-oriented, advanced manufacturing, particularly for MNCs which are not dependent on access to country-specific resources. In addition, their geographical location meant that more or less the same markets could be targeted from affiliates in those countries and from the parent company. Whether an MNC chooses to supply a particular European market from the parent company or from a foreign affiliate, and where it decides to invest in long-term upgrading and development of its plant, will consequently be strongly affected by changes in the relative competitiveness of home and host economies.

Let us compare developments in parent companies and in EC affiliates during the late 1980s.[9] Table 56 shows that manufacturing affiliates in the EC recorded a major expansion of employment in

Table 56 Employment in 'identical' Swedish MNCs, parent companies and manufacturing affiliates, in the EC, by industry, 1986 and 1990

Industry	1986	1990	Change in absolute numbers	Annual change (per cent)
Sweden				
Basic	47,229	66,122	18,893	9
Chemicals	28,928	30,133	1,205	1
Engineering	198,139	163,146	−34,993	−5
EC-12				
Basic	12,011	43,849	31,838	38
Chemicals	5,036	12,291	7,255	25
Engineering	92,840	108,620	15,780	4

Source: IUI database

all three main sectors. Basic industries experienced the most rapid growth, in absolute as well as in relative terms. Here, expansion in the EC was paralleled by strong growth at home as well. While a small upturn was also recorded for parent companies in the chemical sector, engineering displayed a marked decline in Sweden.

Not only was there a major redistribution of production capacity but, as can be seen from Table 57, parent companies in engineering and chemicals were increasingly geared to serving other parts of the European production network. A growing proportion of parent exports comprised supplies of intermediate

Table 57 Share of intermediates in total parent exports to the EC, and in parent exports to manufacturing affiliates in the EC, by industry, 1986 and 1990, per cent

Industry	Exports of intermediates as a share of exports to manufacturing affiliates in the EC		Exports of intermediates as a share of total parent exports	
	1986	1990	1986	1990
Basic industries	79	65	5	3
Chemicals	61	81	10	19
Engineering	50	75	12	33
All industries	53	75	12	18

Source: IUI database

products to manufacturing affiliates. In engineering, the share of intermediates in parent exports to the EC leaped from 12 per cent to 33 percent,[10] and a similar but less accentuated movement is evident in chemicals. In basic industries, on the other hand, intermediates declined as a share of parent exports.

Analyses of productivity in separate parts of MNCs convey further information about the ongoing structural change. Table 58 reports the annual growth of value added per employee in the latter half of the 1980s, for home country operations and affiliated production units in Europe.[11] In basic industries, the parent companies raised value added substantially whereas productivity declined in most other European countries. MNCs in the chemical industry reported improvements in labour productivity in their Swedish operations as well as in most European markets. The experience of engineering was notably different, however. While affiliates throughout the EC and EFTA recorded strong growth, the parent companies recorded average declines in labour productivity of 1.5 per cent per annum. Thus foreign expansion by

Table 58 Average annual changes in value added per employee between 1986 and 1990, by industry, region and selected host countries, 'identical MNCs', per cent

Country	Basic	Chemicals	Engineering
EC			
Belgium	−3.7	+13.3	+10.8
France	−14.6	+2.7	+5.5
Italy	n.a.	+10.9	+16.4
Netherlands	+3.3	−6.5	+0.7
Germany	−3.4	+2.7	+2.7
Denmark	−7.9	+2.4	+2.4
Spain	n.a.	−2.7	+11.2
United Kingdom	+2.1	n.a.	+1.4
EFTA			
Austria	+12.2	+1.0	+17.3
Norway	−1.7	+23.1	+5.4
Finland	+3.4	+5.3	+7.2
Switzerland	−7.2	+0.8	+3.7
Sweden	+5.9	+4.1	−1.5

Note: Only countries for which a sufficiently large number of observations are available are presented in the table.
Source: IUI database

Swedish MNCs in engineering was paralleled not only by a major contraction in operations at home, but also by falling labour productivity among the parents.

For labour productivity to increase faster in foreign subsidiaries than in the Swedish parent companies is no new phenomenon. Between 1965 and 1986, value added per employee consistently rose fastest in foreign units (Swedenborg, 1991). As the absolute level of productivity has generally been higher in home country operations than among foreign affiliates, higher growth abroad has been interpreted as a natural catching-up effect, spurred by transfers of knowledge and technology to the foreign outlets. Swedenborg (1991) concluded, for instance, that the older the affiliate the smaller the gap in labour productivity relative to the parent company.

However, the catching-up effect cannot explain the trend of the late 1980s. In fact, value added per employee in engineering subsidiaries in several EC countries surpassed that of the parent companies in 1990. A similar situation prevailed in chemicals, while MNC home country operations based on natural resources were still considerably more productive compared with EC outlets.[12] In fact, there is a connection between the poor gains in productivity on the part of parents and their increased emphasis on intra-firm trade on supplies of input goods. Regression analysis at the firm level has verified the presence of negative effects on productivity in home operations from the rising share of intermediates in parent exports to EC affiliates (Andersson, 1993b). This suggests that MNCs in engineering relocated late stages of the value-added chain from Sweden to their affiliates in the EC. Strong advances in productivity were recorded parallel with an expansion of output, particularly in German, Italian and British affiliates (Andersson, 1994).

HOME COUNTRY EFFECTS AND RESPONSES

The negative relationship between foreign production and home country exports, the weakening of parent R&D, the lack of perceptible technology transfers homeward from affiliate R&D, and the retreat of productivity at home as intra-firm exports shifted towards intermediates and productivity surged in EC affiliates, are manifestations which strongly suggest that restructuring by Swedish MNCs during the late 1980s accentuated the decline of industry within Sweden.

Table 59 Industrial employment and value added as shares of total
employment and value added in Sweden, 1980, 1985 and 1991

Share of:	1980	1985	1991
Total employment	24.7	22.8	20.0
Total value added	23.6	24.4	20.6

Source: Statistics Sweden, National Accounts

Table 59 shows that the share of manufacturing in total employment fell steadily between 1980 and 1991, with an especially large
contraction in the latter half of the period. Employment growth
occurred mainly in the public sector, in construction and in financial services. In terms of value added, the share of manufacturing
plummeted from 24.4 per cent to 20.6 per cent between 1985 and
1991. In the following years, real domestic investment fell sharply,
unemployment soared to unprecedented levels, public finances
worsened, GDP declined for three consecutive years and real
wages fell. While acknowledging the importance of other factors,
including the worldwide recession, the scale of the contraction
was accentuated by the industrial structure which had evolved.

It is important to consider what processes of further change or
adaptation were spurred by the weakening of industry. Again,
those parts of the economy which were exposed to international
competition were geared to greater emphasis on capital-intensive
and raw-material-based production (NUTEK, 1994). While Swedish
exports of engineering products lost market share worldwide,
basic industries maintained their positions, assisted partly by
successive devaluations of the krona. Among other things, this has
meant that the specialization of Swedish industry *vis-à-vis* its
competitors slid towards sectors characterized by slow growth in
the global economy. The main exception was pharmaceuticals,
which benefited from continuous interactions in knowledge creation among national institutions.

As we saw in Chapter 5, MNCs tend to play a key role in
fostering intangible assets, such as R&D and the training of
people. With technological progress speeding up and spreading
around the world, the need to monitor technological developments on a global scale makes the international networks created
by MNCs even more important for the sourcing and appropria-
tion of foreign technology. While R&D advanced in foreign affiliates, however, we have seen stagnation in the home operations of

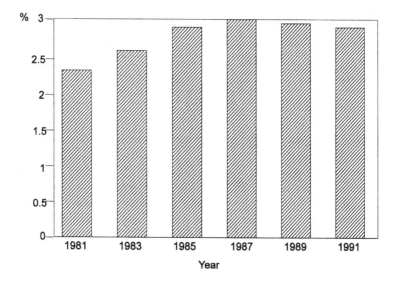

Figure 18 Total expenditure on R&D in Sweden relative to GNP, 1981–91, per cent
Source: Statistics Sweden

Swedish MNCs. In fact, as demonstrated by Figure 18, the trend towards rising R&D expenditures relative to GNP was interrupted in Sweden as a whole, with R&D intensity declining between 1987 and 1991.

The extent to which the home country will benefit from the internationalization of R&D is affected by the parent company's position in the domestic corporate network and by what connections are maintained and upgraded with domestic firms. The extent to which the output from R&D is applied in home country production is of considerable importance in this context. In firms and industries with high R&D intensity, the record of the Swedish parent companies has been weak in terms of both output and productivity growth.

As explained in the preceding chapter, intense interaction and exchange of information between separate functions and parts of a company are crucial for innovating capacity. This is highly relevant to the links between R&D and advanced manufacturing. While some kinds of exchange may easily be handled over great distances, others rely heavily on geographical proximity, e.g. in the form of day-to-day personal contact. A continuous decline in knowledge-intensive manufacturing at home is likely sooner or later to motivate a severe downscaling of domestic R&D. This, in turn, will have far-reaching implications for the prospects of re-vitalizing production.

The dominant influence exerted by a modest number of MNCs which are to varying degrees interlinked with the 'national' Swedish system of industrial R&D, and which also represent important facets of its connections with knowledge creation in the rest of the world, means that the disappearance of certain functions may cause severe dislocation. The effects may spread easily between MNCs as well as to domestic actors, including smaller firms and research institutions. Once the knowledge base at home has been dissipated, each MNC will seek other centres of excellence else-where. In effect, it would mean a reduction in the capacity of the Swedish economy to absorb new technology from abroad, upgrade relevant human competence and foster new activities.

The restructuring among Swedish MNCs has contributed to a heightened awareness that action was needed to improve the competitiveness of the country as an industrial base. One response was the application for membership of the European Community which was submitted on 1 July 1991. From that moment on, outward FDI diminished and the net investment balance changed. In 1993, for the first time for more than 25 years, Sweden experienced a net inflow of FDI. Following the national referendum in November 1994, inward FDI has been given a further boost. In the months immediately following, several major investment decisions were announced by both Swedish-based and foreign companies, some of the latter signalling their intention to use Sweden as regional headquarters of future operations in northern Europe.

There are various explanations for the importance of membership to MNC operations in Sweden. The highly export-oriented Swedish-based companies no longer have to fear discrimination in their major market as a result of decisions taken in Brussels. Although the EEA agreement granted access to the Common Market, border controls were maintained, there was uncertainty concerning the long-term stability of the agreement and non-members were allowed no influence on the formulation of the common rules. This last aspect is important not least in R&D-intensive industries characterized by rapid change and in which new standards are developing continuously. It matters all the more because of the small size of the Swedish economy, and its dependence on intense, vulnerable firm interactions in maintaining or developing the knowledge-based economy.

In addition to membership of the EU, the Swedish authorities have embarked on extensive liberalization of the financial markets, including the conditions for inward FDI. Privatization and deregulation have exposed greater areas of the economy to competition and the social security system has undergone a measure of reform. Major challenges are still looming ahead, however. While historically high real interest rates hamper long-term private investment, the undervalued krona, again, favours sectors which compete chiefly on the basis of price and which generally experience slow growth. Reliance on such activity is likely to be troublesome. Enhanced international competition, and the emergence of new market economies, will hardly improve prospects for success in standardized production. Thus progress in manufacturing based on high added value is warranted in order to avoid a continuous downward adjustment of prices and real wages.

Of course, the welfare implications of MNC behaviour are not determined at the firm level. To the extent that investment and industrial output contract at home, for example, there will be a counteracting price adjustment. Contrary to what is often believed, however, external economies, agglomeration tendencies and the benefits of co-location may result in general equilibrium effects which are magnified rather than diminished by comparison with the firm level. The loss of intensive interaction in knowledge creation cannot be expected to be restored by reduced costs. Thus the restructuring undertaken by MNCs serves as a powerful force which can generate its own lasting impacts on technology, production structures and social welfare, with some smaller countries probably being the most susceptible to change.

7

SUMMARY AND CONCLUDING REMARKS

Relatively little attention has been paid to the impact of FDI which originates in small economies. While the United States used to be the dominant source of FDI, there has been a notable degree of geographical diversification in recent years. As has been highlighted in this book, a number of small economies in Western Europe have substantially increased their share of the world's outward FDI. It is in this category that we find the countries which have the largest stock of outward FDI compared with the size of the economy. There may also be different and more pronounced effects of FDI on small countries compared with large ones. FDI is undertaken by MNCs, which own and control production factors in foreign countries. Such investment not only consists of financial flows but, in particular, involves transfers of intangible assets, e.g. in the form of knowledge about production processes, markets, distribution channels and management. Because assets are intrinsic to the organizations they belong to, the opportunities offered by one actor cannot automatically be replaced by any other. There may be strong interdependence in the behaviour of different firms, implying that small changes in initial conditions may give rise to far-reaching effects. Despite the significance of MNCs, it is far from fully understood how their expansion and restructuring are related to international trade, production, employment and technical progress.

A fundamental reason for this situation is that data on the characteristics and behaviour of individual firms are hard to come by. We have here drawn on a unique data set covering virtually all Swedish MNCs in manufacturing, collected by the Industrial Institute for Economic and Social Research (IUI) in Stockholm since

1965 and updated about every fourth year until 1990. Structures and developments have been studied at the level of individual groups of companies as well as affiliates around the world.

Basic views of the MNC were surveyed in Chapter 2. The two classical models of international organization of operations were recapitulated: horizontal and vertical integration. Vertical integration here refers to the localization of separate stages of the value-added chain in different countries, implying the specialization of activities according to the advantages of each location. In the case of horizontal integration, each affiliate produces primarily for its own specific market, replicating operations in other locations. Of course, this typology represents a very crude simplification, but it has sufficed in the present context. Issues related to the internalization of transactions were further raised, and two alternative modes of entry into foreign markets were pointed out: the establishment of new ventures and the acquisition of existing firms. A new venture allows an MNC to streamline operations in accordance with its own objectives from the start, while acquisition means taking advantage of existing structures but having to adapt them to new needs.

An overview was further provided of locational determinants. It was noted that the location of vertically and horizontally integrated activities is determined in somewhat different ways, but with both affected by pull as well as push factors. While firms based in large economies have been argued to enjoy an advantage in production based on economies of scale, a small domestic market provides firms with a stronger incentive to internationalize production. Where this succeeds, interactions in knowledge creation may be especially important within the small economy. Finally, it was shown that the last decades have seen large shifts in the size and orientation of FDI, with small, industrialized economies becoming a major source of ventures directed towards major markets.

The internationalization of the Swedish economy was reviewed in Chapter 3. Sweden ranked among the leading industrialized countries for many years but has gradually lost its standing. Large firms have been favoured by tax policy, labour market institutions, weak anti-trust legislation, cross-ownership of equity and barriers to inward FDI. Innovations, a strong infrastructure and rich endowments of human capital have paved the way for an expansion of foreign operations by Swedish-based MNCs. Given these prerequisites, the small size of the domestic market has contributed to the advance of Swedish firms abroad.

The flow of outward FDI was magnified in the mid and late 1980s as Swedish MNCs focused on expansion first in the United States and later in the integrating economies of the EC. During the later phase, the internationalization of Swedish MNCs reached an unprecedented level while home operations declined dramatically, with contractionary effects spreading via linkages between companies. While the focus of foreign manufacturing shifted towards the largest economies, activities were scaled down in the developing world. Along with traditional factors such as market size, access to qualified workers and previous trade patterns, location decisions in R&D-intensive industries were significantly affected by agglomeration economics as far as industrialized countries are concerned.

Acquisitions were shown to have gradually but systematically replaced greenfield operations as the predominant entry mode in all industries and in almost all regions, except for East Asia. It was argued that the choice of entry mode is partly determined by the special skills of the investing firm. Firms which are well endowed with their own technology retain a preference for greenfield operations, while a greater ability to organize and synchronize existing technologies favours acquisitions.

In Chapter 4, connections between the internationalization of firms and international trade were studied in closer detail. Swedish exports are strongly influenced by the Swedish-based MNCs, which account for more than half the total. With Sweden being an economy of modest size, the home market has accounted for a gradually declining share of total sales of the Swedish MNCs, reaching barely 20 per cent in 1990. Since the mid 1970s, however, Swedish exports have lost the market share compared with the OECD total, whereas exports have increased dramatically from foreign affiliates of Swedish MNCs. Deliveries back to Sweden have also increased markedly.

Studying the composition of trade within Swedish groups, it was argued that intra-firm trade cannot simply be interpreted as an indicator of vertical integration. While trade in intermediates is primarily related to vertical integration of operations, trade in finished products rather supplements local manufacturing by horizontally integrated affiliates. From 1986 to 1990, the composition of exports from parent companies in Sweden to manufacturing affiliates abroad displayed a notable reorientation from about equal shares of intermediate and finished products to about three-quarters intermediate. At the same time, the swift expansion of exports from foreign affiliates in the EC was found to be related to an increased emphasis on vertical integration, with foreign affiliates playing a decisive role as nodes in networks of operations.

Tracing the behaviour of individual affiliates over time, it was further concluded that acquired affiliates remain less closely linked with parent companies than those established as greenfield operations. An initial difference in the propensity to import finished products from the parent company vanishes over time but, contrary to common assumption, not in the case of imports of intermediates. Finally, significant negative effects were found of foreign production on exports from the home country since the late 1970s. These are partly due to home country exports being replaced by exports from foreign affiliates in the EC.

Impediments to trade knowledge and information at arm's length represent a key factor motivating the existence and expansion of MNCs. The creation and diffusion of technology were analysed in Chapter 5. Swedish MNCs displayed a substantial increase in both R&D expenditure and R&D intensity in the early and mid 1980s. Stagnation occurred in R&D intensity towards the end of the decade, in line with general trends in OECD countries. Relative to MNCs based in larger economies, however, there was a much stronger increase in the share of R&D undertaken abroad. The same observation has been made of Finnish MNCs.

The data further verified that R&D expenditures explain success in MNCs' penetration of foreign markets, with the connection holding for R&D which aims at both product and process innovation. At the same time, the expansion of sales in foreign markets has induced greater product-related R&D in pharmaceuticals, telecommunications and motor vehicles. Extensive R&D has also been associated with a high world market concentration.

Transfers of knowledge generated through R&D in the parent company, partly embodied in intermediate products, show up in the form of higher productivity in affiliates. R&D undertaken in affiliates themselves has not been found to have a direct impact on productivity, but there are significant interactive effects between affiliate R&D and R&D in parent companies. While this indicates a continued emphasis on R&D which upgrades the 'receiver competence' of affiliates with regard to knowledge generated in parent companies, there is also evidence of a shift towards longer-term and more generally applicable R&D abroad. The reasons include an increased need of access to existing foreign technology and the importance of effectively linking R&D and other key functions in the added value chain. At the same time, the prerequisites for R&D weakened in Sweden.

Analysis further showed a close connection between high training expenditure and high R&D intensity. Training expenditures have to a relatively large extent been targeted towards personnel abroad, indicating a great potential for spill-over effects in host countries. In 1990 there was no clear-cut connection between rising training expenditures and labour productivity or wages in the home country. In foreign manufacturing, on the other hand, both wages and productivity were higher in companies with substantial training expenditures. Wages were still higher in Sweden than abroad.

Many of the structural changes occurring among MNCs in the late 1980s centred on affiliates in the EC, where the Single Market was in the process of being established. Connections between regional market integration and MNCs' operations were further analysed in Chapter 6. After the decision to complete the Single Market, the EC attracted greatly expanded FDI from various directions, but with particular emphasis on small economies located on the verge of the Community. In the case of Swedish MNCs, there was a pronounced shift towards vertically integrated units within the emerging Single Market. In EFTA, by contrast, affiliates maintained relatively stronger traits of horizontal integration.

The changes in MNC organization have had far-reaching effects. In the case of Sweden, the country's position outside the integrating Community, coupled with unfavourable conditions at home, gave rise to a restructuring of operations which had a detrimental effect on the Swedish home country. In knowledge-intensive firms and industries, the expansion of operations in the EC was associated with a decline at home, although chemicals, and pharmaceuticals in particular, represent an exception. In basic industries, where many input goods are immobile and production is relatively standardized, expansion occurred both in the EC and in Sweden. These developments are interrelated with the continuous currency depreciation and weakening of real wages.

The variation in performance between industries is reflected in productivity changes. Engineering in particular experienced a decline in labour productivity in the home country and a sharp contraction in the number of employees, while it experienced a strong increase in productivity in EC affiliates. Analyses at the firm level demonstrate the significant negative impact of a shifting orientation in intra-firm exports from the parent company towards the manufacturing affiliates in the EC on productivity in the parent companies.

All in all, these observations suggest that conditions in Europe in the late 1980s brought about a major restructuring of Swedish MNCs, with far-reaching consequences for the home country. Regional trade liberalization within the EC spurred a shift towards international specialization of operations across national borders. Conditions within Sweden together with the country's position outside the integrating Community precipitated both a decline in the volume of operations *and* lower value added in the home country.

These findings point to the importance of devoting more attention to the structures brought about by MNCs' operations rather than just considering FDI. MNCs are able to foster a more sensible and far-reaching adaptation of production to the conditions that prevail in different locations, but small home economies may be particularly susceptible to change. In the face of unfavourable conditions, the restructuring may show up in a rapid deterioration of economic conditions, as adverse effects are magnified by interdependence in firm behaviour.

This is not to say that internationalization should be prevented. Hindering inward as well as outward FDI hampers the pressure for restructuring, with even more awesome consequences down the road. The internationalization of firms sends an increasingly urgent message to the authorities and the general public about the conditions prevailing in an economy. When things are not as they ought to be, it is now being felt more quickly than before, not only through day-to-day fluctuations in financial markets, but also through restructuring of the production apparatus itself, and processes may be difficult to reverse once they have started. Small countries in particular will receive and need to heed the message in time.

In the case of Sweden, barriers against inward FDI, together with a number of institutional and policy-related factors, contributed to heavy reliance on a small number of large and highly internationalized firms. Their competitiveness and concentration of knowledge-creating activities at home represent great assets from the Swedish perspective, but conditions in the 1980s led to weakening linkages at home. Had this trend continued, Sweden would soon have become one of those small countries which find themselves most competitive in standardized rather than knowledge-intensive production.

The momentum set in motion with the creation of the Single Market, including the shift of industrial capacity from the periphery towards the European epicentre, contributed to making most of the small EFTA countries decide to join the project themselves. But, even more than that, the European integration process was itself a reaction to the need to create a basis for common decisions at a time when more and more resource issues leap across national borders. As of the mid 1990s, Sweden – like the other EFTA countries – no longer represents a small country but forms a chunk of the Single Market. Extensive policy reform has been undertaken, productivity has increased markedly in two years and both Swedish and foreign firms are now investing extensively in the country. Still, Sweden is far removed from the position it held a few decades ago, and many doubt that it will ever be there again, just as doubts are being raised about the economic prospects of Europe as a whole. The ultimate outcome will basically hinge on the extent to which the dynamism of the knowledge-creating processes can be restored. This, in turn, depends on mutual benefits being exchanged between companies which are operating and learning worldwide and their counterparts among domestic firms, workers and public institutions which can no longer afford to be rooted solely in a national context.

APPENDIX A
The IUI survey data on Swedish multinational companies

Data on Swedish MNCs have been collected by the Industrial Institute for Economic and Social Research (IUI) about every fourth year since the mid 1960s. The years covered are 1965, 1970, 1974, 1978, 1986 and 1990. The IUI database is not only unique within Sweden. No other information set covers MNCs from a single country equally well in terms of scope or detail. Nowhere else are comprehensive time-series data available on the operations and transactions of individual affiliates. The data provide detailed information on nearly three decades of internationalization, making it possible to consider changes in the organizational structure as well as to trace changes over time in individual MNCs or affiliates around the world.

For the 1990 questionnaire, Thomas Andersson has been responsible for the design and execution of the database. Previous surveys were undertaken by Birgitta Swedenborg. The 1990 question set was updated by Gunnar Fors, who, together with Nicklas Andersson and Torbjörn Fredriksson, also participated in the collection of the 1990 data. Roger Svensson has been responsible for organizing the data and for statistical computations.

Purpose and scope of the surveys

The purpose of the surveys has been to obtain information about and analyse the foreign operations of Swedish industry. Data have been collected on five occasions: 1971, 1975, 1979, 1987 and 1991.[1] The survey covers all Swedish MNCs in manufacturing with more than 50 employees, and with majority-owned producing and/or sales affiliates abroad.[2] Only companies which are registered in Sweden, belong to the manufacturing sector (ISIC 3), and are more than 50 per cent Swedish-owned, have been included. Thus the data do not cover Swedish-based affiliates of foreign MNCs or firms whose major line of operations falls outside manufacturing.[3] Manufacturing firms that are owned by Swedish holding companies have been treated as separate MNCs and as independent of the non-manufacturing part of the corporate group. In principle, all Swedish constituents, i.e. including Swedish-owned subsidiaries in Sweden, are regarded as the parent company. The questions concern the MNC as a whole (Form A) as well as individual foreign manufacturing affiliates (Form B).

Foreign affiliates are defined as companies which are directly or indirectly more than 50 per cent owned by the parent company and which are included in the consolidated accounts of the MNC. A Form B has been filled in for each affiliate performing some kind of manufacturing operations abroad, even if that is not its main activity in value terms. For affiliates which are not engaged in manufacturing but perform, e.g., sales functions, treasury, insurance or transport activities, aggregate information is available on the geographical distribution of the number of employees.

To allow for comparisons over time, the general structure of the IUI question form has remained relatively unchanged over the years. Nevertheless, some modifications should be noted for 1990. First, several questions, which previously drew a distinction between operations in Sweden and abroad, distinguish between operations in the EC and the rest of the world in the 1990 questionnaire. Second, several new questions have been added covering acquisitions undertaken in 1990, training expenditures, marketing expenditures, and market structures (see Form A).

Data collection and rate of response

The population of Swedish MNCs was identified by combining two extracts from the corporate register at Statistics Sweden, covering all large company groups on the one hand and all manufacturing firms with at least 50 employees and with majority-owned affiliates abroad on the other. This information was complemented with companies that were included by Swedenborg *et al.* (1988) in the previous survey but had not shown up in the information from Statistics Sweden. The questionnaire was then distributed to about 500 companies that seemingly matched the criteria for inclusion. Additional information obtained through direct contact with the identified companies, however, led to the exclusion of many entities and narrowed the population to 350 units.

Throughout, the response rate of the IUI surveys has exceeded 90 per cent in terms of number of companies. Concerning the 1990 survey, 329 out of the total of 350 companies (or 94 per cent) replied. Among the respondents, there were 210 without and 119 with manufacturing affiliates abroad. The response rate was 95 per cent for the former and 92 per cent for the latter. In terms of the total value of investment, the coverage is even more extensive, since it was mainly smaller MNCs that declined to reply to the questionnaire. The required information has sometimes been unavailable or very difficult to produce, which has resulted in a lower response rate for certain questions. Still, it practically always remains above 80 per cent. The 119 MNCs with production abroad have completed Form A and Form B for each manufacturing affiliate. The 1990 survey encompasses information concerning 713 foreign manufacturing affiliates.[4]

It should be noted that the gathering of information has become more burdensome for firms over time as Swedish MNCs have grown considerably. For instance, in 1970, the 20 largest MNCs had 11 producing affiliates on average, compared with 25 in 1990. In addition, the organization of business activities has also become more decentralized in terms of financial reporting and information is not always readily available at headquarters. Thus the collection of information has been possible only thanks to tremendous efforts by the participating respondents. Owing to the large number of mergers and acquisitions, it has also become increasingly difficult to monitor MNCs over time.

ACTIVITIES OF SWEDISH MULTINATIONAL ENTERPRISES ABROAD 1990

THE INDUSTRIAL INSTITUTE FOR ECONOMIC
AND SOCIAL RESEARCH
BOX 5501, S-114 85 STOCKHOLM, SWEDEN
TEL: +46 8-783 80 00 (switchboard)
FAX: +46 8-661 79 69
CONTACT PERSONS:
Niklas Arvidsson tel: +46 8-783 84 55
Gunnar Fors tel: +46 8-783 84 51

The forms should be returned before 29 November 1991 to the Industrial
Institute for Economic and Social Research.
NB Please send a copy of your Group Annual Report for 1990.

Form A: Details of the company/group in Sweden and its interests
abroad.
Please read the instructions before filling in the questionnaire.

SECTION I

1. Name and address of the company/parent company:		IUI code (to be filled in by IUI)
. . . .		
. . . .		
2. Contact person:		
Tel: . . . . ext:		
Fax:		
3. The main sector to which the Swedish company/companies in the group belong(s).	Code	
Give the sector code as defined in instructions VIII:1. NB One code only.		

4. List below the industrial enterprises situated in **Sweden** with at least fifty employees which joined/left the group in the period 1986–1990, together with other details of these enterprises.
See instructions III and VIII:1

Company name	Sector (acc. to code in VIII:1)	Year joined	Year left	Number of employees at the time of acquisition /divestment	Number of employees in 1990 (if joined)

Continue on a separate sheet if the table is not large enough.

	Number 1990
5. The number of **production affiliates** abroad. See instructions III. For each such affiliate, form B should be sent in.	

	World wide	of whom in Sweden	of whom in EC countries
6. Total number of group employees in 1990. Average for the year.			

7. Number of employees in **sales affiliates** abroad. See instructions III. Add up the employees of sales affiliates and specify by country.		
Country	IUI code (to be filled in by IUI)	Number of employees 1990

Continue on a separate sheet if the table is not large enough.

8. Details of **other operating affiliates** abroad. See instructions III and VIII:2.			
Country	IUI code (to be filled in by IUI)	Type of business by code in VIII:2	Number of employees 1990

Continue on a separate sheet if the table is not large enough.

	MSEK 1990
9. External revenues of the **entire** group. Invoiced sales plus other operating revenue. All sales within the group should be eliminated.	
10. External revenue of the Swedish part of the group. External revenues in Sweden plus total invoiced exports. Total invoiced exports is defined as external exports plus sales to foreign affiliates. Exports should be valued FOB.	
11. (a) Total invoiced exports of the Swedish part of the group See definition in question 10. **of which** (b) sales to foreign affiliates.	
12. External revenues outside Sweden of the **entire** group. NB Item 12 = items 9 -10 + 11a	
13. Additional information.	

SECTION II. NB Questions 14–39 should only be answered by groups with production affiliates abroad.

14. Allocate the details given in 9, 10 and 11a above among the group's products/product lines (maximum of ten). State in percentages.				
In case of difficulty, first make a rough division of the group's products/product lines (maximum of 10) and then give reasonable estimates in the table. Do not give details of the names of divisions/business areas since this information is asked for in question 33. If you use ISIC codes to classify your products/product lines, please give these codes instead of the names of products/product lines.				
Products/ product lines (or ISIC codes)	IUI code (to be filled in by IUI)	Proportion of total group revenues (question 9) %	Proportion of revenues of the Swedish part of the group (question 10) %	Proportion of exports of the Swedish part of the group (question 11a) %
		Total 100 %	Total 100 %	Total 100 %

15. Allocate the information given in 12 (external revenues outside Sweden of the **entire** group) and 11a (total exports of the Swedish part of the group) among countries/country regions.

The **figures for revenue** relate to the group's total external sales in each country and should include imports to the country and exclude exports from the country. Sales between companies in the group should be eliminated.

The **figures for exports** relate to total exports from Sweden, i.e. both sales to group companies in the country and other exports to the country in question.

Countries/country regions	IUI code (to be filled in by IUI)	External revenues abroad (as in 12) MSEK 1990	Exports from Sweden (as in 11a) MSEK 1990
Belgium			
France			
Italy			
The Netherlands			
Germany (incl. the former East Germany)			
The UK			
Spain			
Portugal			
Greece			
Denmark			
Ireland			
Luxembourg			
Norway			
Finland			
Switzerland			
Austria			
Rest of Western Europe			
The Soviet Union			
Rest of Eastern Europe (excl. the former East Germany)			
The USA			
Canada			
Latin America			
of which Argentina			

Brazil			
Mexico			
Africa			
of which South Africa			
Asia			
of which Japan			
Australia and New Zealand			
Total Should be the same as the replies to questions 12 and 11a.		(= 12)	(= 11a)

	MSEK 1990
16. (a) Total revenues of the **Swedish** part of the group from licences, patents, royalties, know-how and management fees Including contributions to cover the costs of R & D and central administration. Excluding payments between Swedish companies in the group. Make reasonable estimates.	
of which (b) income from foreign affiliates.	
(c) income from other foreign companies.	
17. (a) Expenditure of the **entire** group on licences, patents, royalties and know-how. Excluding payments between companies in the group. Make reasonable estimates.	
of which (b) payments to countries other than Sweden.	

Answer questions 18–22 for **the group** as a whole and in relation to how much of this total amount concerns **Sweden** and **EC countries**.	MSEK 1990		
	The group as a whole	of which in Sweden	of which in EC countries
18. (a) Capital expenditure by the group			
Relates to gross investments in machinery, equipment and buildings and should include the initial values of machinery, equipment and buildings for companies acquired in 1990. Acquired companies refers to companies in which the group has acquired at least 50 % of the share capital.			
of which (b) initial values of **machinery, equipment and buildings** for companies acquired in 1990.			
19. Initial values of **total assets** for companies acquired in 1990.			
See question 18(a) for the definition of acquired companies.			
20. Group expenditure on training.			
Relates to company-specific and general training arranged or financed by the group for the employees. Make reasonable estimates.			
21. Group expenditure on marketing.			
Relates to the group's internal costs for the marketing department etc. and to external costs, such as the purchasing of marketing services and advertising costs. Market investments should also be included, i.e. expenses of a long-term nature such as the cultivation of markets. Make reasonable estimates.			
22. Group expenditure on research and development (R & D).			
Excluding payments between companies in the group. R & D expenditure refers to both current expenses and depreciation on capital equipment for R & D. Both R & D carried out in-house and R & D commissioned by the affiliate from a third party should be included. In the Sweden and EC columns, state the proportion of total R & D carried out in Sweden and in EC countries.			
(As defined by Statistics Sweden, see instructions VIII:3.)			

Answer questions 23, 27–29 and 32 for the group as a whole and in relation to how much of this total amount concerns the Swedish part of the group and EC affiliates. The other questions on this page should only be answered for the group as a whole.	MSEK 1990		
	Group as a whole	of which in the Swedish part of the group	of which in EC group affiliates
23. The value of fixed assets Relates to machinery, equipment and buildings. (a) book value (planned residual value)			
(b) estimated replacement value			
24. Total liabilities (excl. untaxed reserves)		XXXXX	XXXXX
25. Untaxed reserves		XXXXX	XXXXX
26. Total equity		XXXXX	XXXXX
27. Total assets (book value)			

28. Operating income before depreciation			
29. Depreciation according to plan			
30. Total interest expense		XXXXX	XXXXX
31. Income after financial income and expense		XXXXX	XXXXX

32. Total expenditure on wages and salaries (incl. fringe benefits). See instructions VIII:4.			

33. Allocate the information in the table below among the group's five largest divisions/business areas in terms of revenue **and** a residual item for other divisions/business areas (where you have more than five divisions) **and** one item for operations common to the group (i.e. operations which fall outside the divisions, e.g. head office, group management, holding company, real estate management and financing). State in percentages.

Div 1 + 2 + 3 + 4 + 5 + residual item + common to the group = 100 %. If you have fewer than five divisions, leave the extra boxes for the divisions and the residual item empty.

Make reasonable estimates in cases where the information is not easy to allocate.

	Name of division/business area	IUI code (to be filled in by IUI)	Total group revenues (question 9)	Revenues of the Swedish part of the group (question 10)
Div 1			%	%
Div 2			%	%
Div 3			%	%
Div 4			%	%
Div 5			%	%
Residual item for other divisions	XXXXXXX		%	%
Common to the group	XXXXXXX		%	%
Total	XXXXXXX		100 %	100 %

Question 33 continued. NB The same divisions as above.

	Total assets (question 27)		Operating income before depreciation (question 28)		Total expenditure on wages and salaries (question 32)	
	Group as a whole	of which in Sweden	**Group as a whole**	of which in Sweden	**Group as a whole**	of which in Sweden
Div 1	%	%	%	%	%	%
Div 2	%	%	%	%	%	%
Div 3	%	%	%	%	%	%
Div 4	%	%	%	%	%	%
Div 5	%	%	%	%	%	%

Residual item for other divisions	%	%	%	%	%	%
Common to the group	%	%	%	%	%	%
Total	100 %	100 %	100 %	100 %	100 %	100 %

	Worldwide	of which in Sweden	of which in EC countries
34. The number of those employed in operations common to the group. See question 33 for a definition of this activity.			

35. List the names of the group's **Swedish production enterprises** in divisions 1–5 (and the residual item) as in question 33. Limit the details to industrial enterprises having at least 200 employees. In the table give the company names by divisions.

Continue on a separate sheet if the table is not large enough.

	IUI code (to be filled in by IUI)	Names of companies in each division	IUI code (to be filled in by IUI)
Div 1			
Div 2			
Div 3			
Div 4			
Div 5			
Residual item for other divisions			

EVALUATION QUESTIONS

36. Give the names of the **four** largest (in terms of revenue) manufacturers in the world in each sector for your **two** largest divisions/business areas (the **two** largest divisions in terms of revenue in question 33). Make reasonable estimates of the world market shares of these manufacturers in each sector.

If you yourself are one of these manufacturers, write the name of your own group and your market share on one line and corresponding information for your three largest competitors on the remaining three lines. In cases where it is difficult to identify a sector, competitors and market shares for your two largest divisions, please make **reasonable estimates,** based on the main sector classification/products of the divisions.

Division 1: the largest in question 33 (= sector 1)		
Names of the four largest manufacturers in sector 1	Market share sector 1	IUI code (to be filled in by IUI)
1.	%	
2.	%	
3.	%	
4.	%	

Division 2: the second largest in question 33 (= sector 2)		
Names of the four largest manufacturers in sector 2	Market share sector 2	IUI code (to be filled in by IUI)
1.	%	
2.	%	
3.	%	
4.	%	

37. Give a breakdown of the revenues of the manufacturers identified in question 36 by region.

Relates to the revenues of manufacturers for the products of each sector. Make reasonable estimates and give percentages.

The four largest manufacturers in sector 1 (as in 36 above)	Breakdown of revenues by region			IUI code (to be filled in by IUI)
	Europe	North America	East Asia	
1	%	%	%	
2	%	%	%	
3	%	%	%	
4	%	%	%	

The four largest manufacturers in sector 2 (as in 36 above)	Breakdown of revenues by region			IUI code (to be filled in by IUI)
	Europe	North America	East Asia	
1	%	%	%	
2	%	%	%	
3	%	%	%	
4	%	%	%	

	Division 1		Division 2	
38. For the two divisions in question 36, state whether responsibility for profitability is required globally, regionally and/or locally. Place a cross under Yes or No.	Yes	No	Yes	No
(a) Globally				
(b) Regionally (e.g. the North American business, regardless of exactly how this region is defined).				
(c) Locally (e.g. national market or other area for which an organizational unit is responsible.				

39. For each of the activities named below, state to what extent the group co-ordinates these activities internationally. Answer for the group as a whole and for the two divisions in question 36.

State the degree of international co-ordination as a percentage between 0 and 100, where 0 relates to total absence of international co-ordination and 100 relates to complete international co-ordination.

Activity	The group as a whole	Division 1	Division 2
Manufacturing			
Research and development			
Marketing			

ACTIVITIES OF SWEDISH MULTINATIONAL ENTERPRISES ABROAD 1990

THE INDUSTRIAL INSTITUTE FOR ECONOMIC
AND SOCIAL RESEARCH
BOX 5501, S-114 85 STOCKHOLM, SWEDEN
TEL: +46 8-783 80 00 (switchboard)
FAX: +46 8-661 79 69
CONTACT PERSONS:
Niklas Arvidsson tel: +46 8-783 84 55
Gunnar Fors tel: +46 8-783 84 51

The forms should be returned before 29 November 1991 to the Industrial Institute for Economic and Social Research.

Form B: Details of the production affiliate abroad.

Please read the instructions before filling in the questionnaire.

	IUI code (to be filled in by IUI)
1. Name of the affiliate: .... Country:.....................................	
Parent company of the group:	
The affiliate belongs to the following division/business area:... .... If the affiliate belongs to more than one division, state which ones and estimate the proportion of the affiliate's revenue attributable to each division. Use the same names as in question 33 of form A.	
2. (a) Since what year has the affiliate been a production company of the group?	....
(b) Was the affiliate a sales company of the group before the year mentioned above?	yes ..... no ...
(c) Did the affiliate operate as a production company of another group before the year mentioned?	yes ..... no ...

155

	MSEK 1990
3. (a) Total invoiced sales Sales should be stated net, i.e. after deductions for revenue tax, discounts and returns.	
of which (b) goods made or assembled by the affiliate. Make a reasonable assessment. The difference between 3a and 3b is made up of goods which are resold only, without being processed by the affiliate.	
4. (a) Total invoiced exports of 3 (a) Including exports to other companies in the group. Exports should be valued FOB.	
of which (b) exports to Sweden.	
(c) exports to Swedish companies in the group. Make reasonable estimates.	
5. (a) Imports of goods from the Swedish companies in the group Imports should be valued FOB Sweden. Make reasonable estimates.	
of which (b) goods for resale with no processing by the affiliate.	
(c) goods for processing by the affiliate.	

6. Make-up of the affiliate's production as in 3 (b) above. State the principal products/product lines made by the affiliate, together with the proportion of production held by each.

See question 14 of form A. If possible, use the same names of products/product lines as in question A:14. Give ISIC codes if you used these codes in question A:14 instead of the names of products/product lines.

Products/product lines (or ISIC codes)	IUI code (to be filled in by IUI)	Share of total production (as in 3b) %
		Total 100 %

	MSEK 1990
7. Capital expenditure. Relates to gross investments in machinery, equipment and buildings.	
8. Expenditure on research and development (R & D). Excluding payments between group companies. R & D expenditure refers to both current expenses and depreciation on capital equipment for R & D. Both R & D carried out in-house and R & D commissioned by the affiliate from a third party should be included (as defined by Statistics Sweden, see instructions VIII:3).	

	MSEK 1990
9. The value of fixed assets Relates to machinery, equipment and buildings. (a) book value (planned residual value)	
(b) estimated replacement value	
10. (a) Total liabilities (excl. untaxed reserves)	
of which (b) long-term debt to the Swedish companies in the group.	
11. Untaxed reserves	
12. Total equity	
13. Total assets (book value)	
14. Proportion of the share capital owned See instructions VIII:5. (a) directly and indirectly by the parent company of the group.	%
(b) directly by the Swedish companies in the group.	%

	MSEK 1990
15. Operating income before depreciation	
16. Depreciation according to plan	
17. Total interest expense	
18. Income after financial interest and expense	

19. (a) Net income for 1990 (after tax).	
(b) Total dividend declared on the net income for 1990.	
(c) Dividend remitted to the Swedish companies of the group (excl. withholding tax). Relates to remittance of the net income for 1990, regardless of when the actual remittance was made.	

	Number 1990
20. Total expenditure on wages and salaries (incl. fringe benefits). See instructions VIII:4.	
21. Number of employees. Average number of employees during the year.	

22. Additional information.

APPENDIX B

The following tables are updated from Swedenborg *et al.* (1988), appendix C. Notations in parentheses at the end of each table heading refer to table numbers in that book. Industries in Tables B.1–7 refer to the industry classification of the affiliates. The metals industry includes both the iron and steel and the metal products industries. There may be differences in the figures for individual industries in Tables B.1–7 compared with Swedenborg *et al.* (1988), as the industry category of some affiliates has been adjusted.

B.1. Total assets in foreign manufacturing affiliates, by industry, 1960–90. Current prices (MSEK). (C.1)

B.2. Number of employees in foreign manufacturing affiliates, by industry, 1960–90. (C.1)

B.3. Total sales in foreign manufacturing affiliates, by industry, 1965–90. Current prices (MSEK). (C.2a)

B.4. Exports from foreign manufacturing affiliates, by industry, 1965–90. Current prices (MSEK). (C.2a)

B.5. Exports to Sweden from foreign manufacturing affiliates, by industry, 1965–90. Current prices (MSEK). (C.2b)

B.6. Imports from Sweden to foreign manufacturing affiliates, by industry, 1965–90. Current prices (MSEK). (C.2b)

B.7. Imports of intermediate goods from Sweden to foreign manufacturing affiliates, by industry, 1965–90. Current prices (MSEK).

B.8. Total assets in foreign manufacturing affiliates, by country and region, 1960–90. Current prices (MSEK). (C.3)

B.9. Number of employees in foreign manufacturing affiliates, by country and region, 1960–90. (C.3)

B.10. Total sales in foreign manufacturing affiliates, by region, 1965–90. Current prices (MSEK). (C.4a)

B.11. Exports from foreign manufacturing affiliates, by region, 1965–90. Current prices (MSEK). (C.4a)

B.12. Exports to Sweden from foreign manufacturing affiliates, by region, 1965–90. Current prices (MSEK). (C.4b)

B.13. Imports from Sweden to foreign manufacturing affiliates, by region, 1965–90. Current prices (MSEK). (C.4b)

B.14. Imports of intermediate goods from Sweden to foreign manufacturing affiliates, by region, 1965–90. Current prices (MSEK).

B.15. Number of employees in foreign sales affiliates of all Swedish multinational firms, by country and region, 1965–90. (C.5)

B.16. Number of employees in foreign sales affiliates of Swedish multinational firms with production abroad, by country and region, 1965–90. (C.6)

B.17. Total Swedish exports, by region, 1965–90. Current prices. (C.8)

Table B.1. Total assets in foreign manufacturing affiliates, by industry, 1960–90. Current prices (MSEK)

	No. of affiliates (1990)	1960	1965	1970	1974	1978	1986	1990
Food	5	12	28	137	198	354	2,386	621
Textiles	9	5	13	79	158	206	277	715
Paper and pulp	41	0	298	1,046	2,104	2,982	4,361	33,453
Paper products	37	11	88	416	1,093	2,531	16,004	16,956
Chemicals	137	534	865	1,279	1,690	3,037	14,717	33,633
Metals	183	418	922	2,015	3,493	6,575	10,523	26,690
Machinery	112	1,925	3,819	6,296	8,430	15,642	33,029	40,221
Electronics	121	694	1,437	2,728	6,524	9,055	45,904	47,789
Transport	23	55	189	545	1,806	5,029	10,911	18,828
Other	45	180	319	856	1,845	1,847	4,742	6,790
All industries	713	3,834	7,979	15,396	27,342	47,257	142,854	225,696

Table B.2. Number of employees in foreign manufacturing affiliates, by industry, 1960–90

	1960	1965	1970	1974	1978	1986	1990
Food	205	568	1,967	1,562	2,174	3,807	679
Textiles	240	704	3,367	5,844	4,583	2,702	3,008
Paper and pulp	0	1,772	4,104	6,740	8,707	6,721	32,863
Paper products	111	1,508	3,820	6,438	12,314	20,792	22,837
Chemicals	21,908	23,852	24,611	23,236	16,585	28,737	31,433
Metals	7,133	11,537	18,819	24,910	28,414	24,470	43,191
Machinery	49,843	66,898	73,633	69,792	66,496	61,987	63,315
Electronics	20,150	31,411	37,377	57,974	60,002	82,748	87,194
Transport	1,117	2,910	4,366	11,267	18,057	16,436	22,639
Other	4,804	6,132	10,023	13,348	9,817	11,423	9,149
All industries	105,511	147,292	182,087	221,111	227,149	259,823	316,308

Table B.3. Total sales in foreign manufacturing affiliates, by industry, 1965–90. Current prices (MSEK)

	1965	1970	1974	1978	1986	1990
Food	25	170	218	630	3,371	517
Textiles	21	102	300	443	531	1,204
Paper and pulp	181	547	1,854	2,848	5,125	39,661
Paper products	125	526	1,521	3,178	17,548	20,847
Chemicals	998	1,383	2,148	4,060	17,747	30,282
Metals	1,057	2,547	4,539	8,094	17,217	40,978
Machinery	3,889	6,259	9,441	15,837	37,515	49,595
Electronics	1,597	2,536	6,290	10,966	47,963	69,368
Transport	296	934	3,058	8,409	28,449	40,902
Other	301	866	1,973	2,525	6,424	8,280
All industries	8,489	15,869	31,342	56,989	181,890	301,633

Table B.4. Exports from foreign manufacturing affiliates, by industry, 1965–90. Current prices (MSEK)

	1965	*1970*	*1974*	*1978*	*1986*	*1990*
Food	8	12	42	217	480	173
Textiles	13	79	227	288	454	861
Paper and pulp	72	197	586	640	1,638	14,820
Paper products	13	62	175	635	3,941	4,954
Chemicals	63	131	317	425	2,673	4,700
Metals	84	280	729	864	2,604	9,752
Machinery	531	1,225	2,665	4,765	12,285	19,649
Electronics	84	228	725	1,226	7,741	12,917
Transport	56	369	1,286	4,307	13,895	22,760
Other	88	189	505	485	1,975	541
All industries	1,012	2,772	7,257	13,854	47,686	91,128

Table B.5. Exports to Sweden from foreign manufacturing affiliates, by industry, 1965–90. Current prices (MSEK)

	1965	*1970*	*1974*	*1978*	*1986*	*1990*
Food	8	8	4	22	140	100
Textiles	9	62	161	172	257	185
Paper and pulp	0	15	0	6	76	356
Paper products	0	9	34	139	438	536
Chemicals	7	27	58	135	435	649
Metals	7	38	212	105	488	710
Machinery	58	108	263	464	1,234	2,137
Electronics	25	62	161	369	1,164	1,945
Transport	0	26	38	458	3,832	8,307
Other	5	41	79	79	232	68
All industries	118	395	1,010	1,949	8,295	14,991

Table B.6. Imports from Sweden to foreign manufacturing affiliates, by industry, 1965–90. Current prices (MSEK)

	1965	*1970*	*1974*	*1978*	*1986*	*1990*
Food	0	15	9	22	158	22
Textiles	3	17	21	56	71	117
Paper and pulp	5	45	187	190	472	1,170
Paper products	12	59	202	294	1,288	1,359
Chemicals	37	92	217	515	1,421	1,591
Metals	399	910	1,360	2,297	3,866	6,183
Machinery	330	564	831	1,470	2,871	2,401
Electronics	191	367	1,316	1,408	4,801	7,567
Transport	123	340	1,186	3,071	9,133	12,185
Other	9	21	49	64	400	502
All industries	1,110	2,432	5,378	9,387	24,481	33,095

Table B.7. Imports of intermediate goods from Sweden to foreign manufacturing affiliates, by industry, 1965–90. Current prices (MSEK)

	1965	*1970*	*1974*	*1978*	*1986*	*1990*
Food	0	1	1	1	37	0
Textiles	2	11	17	28	46	101
Paper and pulp	5	41	187	183	413	1,125
Paper products	9	32	113	147	578	444
Chemicals	8	19	53	256	784	1,125
Metals	82	174	351	511	1,244	1,964
Machinery	128	185	375	409	401	348
Electronics	64	122	410	404	1,771	4,640
Transport	118	308	849	2,308	6,064	11,518
Other	5	11	12	30	351	61
All industries	420	903	2,368	4,277	11,689	21,325

Table B.8. Total assets in foreign manufacturing affiliates, by country and region, 1960–90. Current prices (MSEK)

	No. of affiliates (1990)	1960	1965	1970	1974	1978	1986	1990
All developed countries	633	3,340	6,940	13,111	23,174	40,151	129,878	210,164
EC-6	241	1,593	3,799	7,306	13,636	22,564	51,856	99,497
Belgium	17	146	314	821	1,766	2,611	5,189	10,651
France	53	437	819	1,608	3,391	4,819	9,779	14,004
Italy	46	152	969	1,426	2,422	2,958	16,991	24,146
Netherlands	35	93	259	685	1,287	3,860	5,236	7,661
Germany	90	765	1,438	2,767	4,770	8,316	14,658	43,036
EC-3	139	468	787	1,611	2,491	5,349	13,996	31,186
Denmark	46	71	137	623	1,068	1,724	5,374	8,433
United Kingdom	87	397	649	990	1,396	3,541	8,217	21,868
Ireland	6	0	0	0	27	84	405	885
EC-south	33	37	77	625	1,149	1,413	4,307	12,200
Portugal	10	22	31	429	481	496	1,401	2,861
Spain	21	13	41	190	649	887	2,906	9,123
Greece	2	2	5	5	19	29	0	216
EFTA	89	258	587	1,124	1,609	2,932	10,288	14,290
Norway	34	74	220	499	472	811	3,963	3,735
Finland	32	98	218	343	790	1,192	3,809	3,512
Switzerland	10	11	16	16	72	434	1,113	1,630
Austria	13	75	132	266	275	494	1,403	5,413
North America	100	813	1,320	1,801	2,847	6,047	45,182	46,791
United States	82	662	917	1,094	1,817	4,820	41,981	42,591
Canada	18	151	403	706	1,030	1,228	3,202	4,201
Other developed countries	31	172	371	645	1,441	1,847	4,249	6,200
South Africa	2	72	147	242	362	424	374	349
Japan	10	0	0	0	121	283	835	1,885
Australia	14	100	206	376	926	1,083	2,575	3,655
New Zealand	3	0	15	17	21	30	421	240
Other	2	0	4	10	12	27	44	70
All developing countries	80	494	1,039	2,285	4,168	7,106	12,975	15,532
Africa	6	3	87	72	123	20	41	154
Asia	23	169	297	302	442	583	1,702	2,462
India	4	123	37	45	122	255	793	1,303
Other	19	46	260	257	320	329	909	1,159
Latin America	51	323	654	1,911	3,604	6,502	11,233	12,917

Argentina	7	43	80	281	288	606	995	1,106
Brazil	17	201	388	1,082	2,395	4,378	5,913	7,143
Colombia	4	10	18	75	104	213	455	469
Mexico	11	46	107	277	519	520	2,671	2,925
Other	12	23	62	194	298	787	1,199	1,273
All regions	713	3,834	7,979	15,396	27,342	47,257	142,854	225,696

Table B.9. Number of employees in foreign manufacturing affiliates, by country and region, 1960–90

	1960	1965	1970	1974	1978	1986	1990
All developed countries	87,608	120,196	145,044	175,375	182,112	214,929	274,209
EC-6	48,645	68,794	82,649	97,229	92,355	93,000	114,182
Belgium	2,579	4,596	5,944	8,242	9,549	9,036	9,881
France	13,666	16,116	21,196	28,797	23,392	18,024	18,431
Italy	3,768	15,876	15,526	17,919	15,619	30,226	29,460
Netherlands	2,096	3,496	7,450	8,380	13,159	7,905	11,330
Germany	26,536	28,710	32,533	33,891	30,636	27,809	45,080
EC-3	14,533	17,496	20,873	23,805	30,209	27,878	48,994
Denmark	2,459	2,817	6,946	7,736	7,469	10,669	11,615
United Kingdom	12,074	14,679	13,927	15,583	21,761	16,167	36,463
Ireland	0	0	0	486	979	1,042	916
EC-south	1,901	2,457	6,343	11,104	10,555	11,436	15,564
Portugal	1,179	1,423	3,959	4,905	3,876	3,450	3,925
Spain	659	971	2,321	5,959	6,539	7,986	10,952
Greece	63	63	63	240	140	0	687
EFTA	6,885	11,285	14,762	15,246	15,818	17,771	15,520
Norway	1,810	3,909	5,338	3,638	3,366	5,946	4,709
Finland	2,760	4,462	5,870	8,152	7,822	7,538	3,900
Switzerland	368	359	253	582	1,971	1,761	1,774
Austria	1,947	2,555	3,301	2,873	2,659	2,526	5,137
North America	12,368	14,638	12,316	17,024	24,940	53,678	71,166
United States	9,651	12,483	9,795	13,345	20,859	49,523	66,500
Canada	2,717	2,155	2,521	3,679	4,081	4,155	4,666
Other developed countries	3,276	5,526	8,101	10,967	8,235	11,166	8,783
South Africa	1,713	2,490	2,643	3,342	2,560	1,967	1,092
Japan	0	0	0	214	460	681	1,261
Australia	1,563	2,633	5,042	6,621	4,368	6,506	6,008
New Zealand	0	343	330	318	393	1,530	218
Other	0	60	86	472	454	482	204

All developing countries	17,903	27,096	37,043	45,736	45,037	44,894	42,099
Africa	174	574	569	612	156	491	473
Asia	10,051	13,565	13,982	15,590	5,907	13,222	11,000
India	7,985	2,146	1,763	3,092	2,609	8,548	6,445
Other	2,066	11,419	12,219	12,498	3,298	4,674	4,555
Latin America	7,678	12,957	22,492	29,534	38,974	31,181	30,626
Argentina	1,241	1,377	2,674	2,559	3,674	2,896	2,671
Brazil	4,764	8,065	12,981	19,892	24,019	15,012	14,024
Colombia	319	531	1,048	930	3,277	1,940	2,059
Mexico	939	1,899	3,268	4,569	4,500	6,880	6,893
Other	415	1,085	2,521	1,584	3,504	4,453	4,979
All regions	105,511	147,292	182,087	221,111	227,149	259,823	316,308

Table B.10. Total sales in foreign manufacturing affiliates, by region, 1965–90. Current prices (MSEK)

	1965	1970	1974	1978	1986	1990
Developed countries	7,468	13,984	27,489	50,378	168,834	282,997
EC-6	3,883	8,029	15,737	28,131	76,505	138,115
EC-3	904	1,778	3,245	7,132	18,905	43,205
EC-south	69	366	1,010	1,306	4,893	13,706
EFTA	707	1,316	2,393	4,011	13,120	16,043
North America	1,520	1,847	3,462	7,505	48,519	62,636
Other developed countries	385	648	1,642	2,294	6,892	9,293
Developing countries	1,022	1,885	3,853	6,611	13,057	18,636
Africa	42	48	150	30	68	304
Asia	394	430	572	592	1,853	3,102
Latin America	586	1,407	3,131	5,988	11,136	15,230
All regions	8,489	15,869	31,342	56,989	181,890	301,633

Table B.11. Exports from foreign manufacturing affiliates, by region, 1965–90. Current prices (MSEK)

	1965	1970	1974	1978	1986	1990
Developed countries	973	2,687	7,036	13,309	46,146	89,509
EC-6	645	1,796	4,870	9,833	31,081	64,263
EC-3	111	270	735	1,350	5,141	8,933
EC-south	16	197	320	302	2,214	2,403
EFTA	82	220	555	983	3,383	5,293
North America	117	196	405	751	3,948	7,925
Other developed countries	2	8	152	90	379	692
Developing countries	39	85	221	545	1,540	1,619
Africa	36	41	134	0	0	0
Asia	0	9	2	41	151	83
Latin America	3	35	85	504	1,389	1,536
All regions	1,012	2,772	7,257	13,854	47,686	91,128

Table B.12. Exports to Sweden from foreign manufacturing affiliates, by region, 1965–90. Current prices (MSEK)

	1965	1970	1974	1978	1986	1990
Developed countries	117	384	996	1,907	8,251	14,659
EC-6	40	126	347	985	5,375	10,713
EC-3	32	72	225	311	1,259	1,418
EC-south	9	76	119	78	224	357
EFTA	32	94	269	479	1,198	1,156
North America	4	14	16	23	142	837
Other developed countries	0	3	19	31	53	178
Developing countries	1	10	14	42	44	333
Africa	1	7	0	0	0	0
Asia	0	1	0	9	1	8
Latin America	0	2	14	33	43	325
All regions	118	395	1,010	1,949	8,295	14,991

Table B.13. Imports from Sweden to foreign manufacturing affiliates, by region, 1965–90. Current prices (MSEK)

	1965	1970	1974	1978	1986	1990
Developed countries	1,036	2,216	4,453	8,538	22,735	30,592
EC-6	457	1,097	2,067	4,452	11,702	17,298
EC-3	145	319	660	1,578	2,963	4,347
EC-south	12	55	139	116	499	1,419
EFTA	93	298	577	746	1,905	1,424
North America	203	327	516	1,127	4,092	3,849
Other developed countries	126	121	493	518	1,574	2,255
Developing countries	74	216	925	849	1,747	2,504
Africa	0	2	1	5	10	3
Asia	14	24	104	140	130	848
Latin America	60	190	820	704	1,607	1,653
All regions	1,110	2,432	5,378	9,387	24,481	33,095

Table B.14. Imports of intermediate goods from Sweden to foreign manufacturing affiliates, by region, 1965–90. Current prices (MSEK)

	1965	1970	1974	1978	1986	1990
Developed countries	394	825	1,920	3,820	10,723	19,896
EC-6	212	471	1,008	2,174	6,3970	12,2248
EC-3	33	91	205	789	1,095	2,984
EC-south	2	20	91	51	224	903
EFTA	26	67	132	129	572	372
North America	80	136	294	420	1,615	2,193
Other developed countries	40	41	191	256	846	1,197
Developing countries	26	78	448	457	966	1,429
Africa	0	0	1	2	8	0
Asia	4	13	80	86	66	282
Latin America	22	65	368	369	891	1,147
All regions	420	903	2,368	4,277	11,689	21,325

Table B.15. Number of employees in foreign sales affiliates of all Swedish multinational firms, by country and region, 1965–90

	1965	1970	1974	1978	1986	1990
All developed countries	20,900	36,008	47,307	45,834	70,614	57,788
EC-6	7,954	13,386	20,883	18,800	23,655	23,414
Belgium	834	1,117	1,281	1,524	2,259	5,521
France	1,498	2,819	3,747	3,920	5,494	3,064
Italy	3,248	4,591	6,523	5,658	5,145	6,799
Netherlands	527	1,082	1,981	1,745	3,153	3,278
Germany	1,847	3,777	7,351	5,953	7,604	4,752
EC-3	5,160	8,077	8,289	6,733	13,337	10,476
Denmark	1,850	2,714	4,195	3,622	5,164	3,448
United Kingdom	3,139	5,172	4,003	2,997	7,998	6,381
Ireland	171	191	91	114	175	647
EC-south	1,024	1,562	1,886	1,642	2,265	3,796
Portugal	338	673	728	536	563	440
Spain	523	717	984	859	1,480	3,204
Greece	163	172	174	247	222	152
EFTA	3,793	6,499	9,535	9,276	13,967	9,824
Norway	1,472	2,653	3,755	3,961	5,398	3,449
Finland	1,323	1,900	2,730	2,614	4,705	3,189
Switzerland	693	1,359	1,926	1,634	2,322	1,793
Austria	305	587	1,124	1,067	1,542	1,394
North America	1,520	2,786	3,889	4,425	9,873	6,578
United States	1,220	2,273	2,873	3,061	8,778	5,227
Canada	300	513	1,016	1,364	1,095	1,351
Other developed countries	1,374	3,629	2,723	4,829	7,433	3,590
South Africa	592	1,479	1,253	472	281	61
Japan	119	322	471	1,926	3,282	1,001
Australia and New Zealand	598	1,742	893	2,282	3,667	1,864
Other	65	86	106	149	201	664
Eastern Europe	75	69	102	129	84	110
All developing countries	3,927	6,723	8,481	7,357	11,462	14,413
Africa	122	229	269	544	496	338
Asia	877	1,351	1,778	2,233	8,066	8,156
Latin America	2,928	5,143	6,434	4,580	2,900	5,919
Argentina	260	452	360	292	271	74
Brazil	311	542	981	745	87	1,963
Chile	187	256	345	159	335	344
Colombia	714	990	988	68	158	113
Mexico	448	1,193	1,488	1,757	851	736
Peru	398	384	428	679	469	624

Venezuela	123	1,045	1,358	221	267	278
Other	149	281	486	659	462	1,787
All regions	24,827	42,731	55,788	53,191	82,076	72,201

Table B.16. Number of employees in foreign sales affiliates for Swedish firms with production abroad, by country and region, 1965–90

	1965	1970	1974	1978	1986	1990
All developed countries	16,846	32,704	41,664	45,834	61,538	53,330
EC-6	6,998	12,721	19,234	18,800	21,137	22,155
Belgium	758	1,117	1,115	1,524	2,093	5,480
France	1,471	2,755	3,471	3,920	4,897	2,731
Italy	3,206	4,584	6,523	5,658	5,062	6,733
Netherlands	452	1,082	1,500	1,745	2,798	3,136
Germany	1,111	3,183	6,625	5,953	6,287	4,075
EC-3	3,467	7,405	6,957	6,733	10,952	9,029
Denmark	1,543	2,570	3,662	3,622	4,356	2,893
United Kingdom	1,753	4,644	3,204	2,997	6,426	5,489
Ireland	171	191	91	114	170	647
EC-south	868	1,554	1,732	1,642	2,177	3,754
Portugal	236	673	728	536	560	438
Spain	506	717	811	859	1,408	3,164
Greece	126	164	193	247	209	152
EFTA	2,887	5,920	8,702	9,276	12,151	8,766
Norway	1,027	2,197	3,257	3,961	4,206	2,884
Finland	1,192	1,816	2,497	2,614	4,241	2,813
Switzerland	457	1,335	1,857	1,634	2,234	1,750
Austria	211	572	1,091	1,067	1,470	1,320
North America	1,205	2,213	3,351	4,425	8,918	6,050
United States	966	1,823	2,491	3,061	8,006	4,765
Canada	239	390	860	1,364	912	1,285
Other developed countries	1,346	2,822	1,586	4,829	6,119	3,522
South Africa	592	1,479	366	472	281	61
Japan	107	310	294	1,926	1,951	1,001
Australia	459	778	575	1,980	3,000	1,625
New Zealand	138	173	233	302	602	171
Other	50	82	118	149	285	664
Eastern Europe	75	69	102	129	84	54
All developing countries	3,069	6,507	7,669	7,357	11,175	14,370
Africa	122	229	269	544	496	334
Asia	746	1,231	1,198	2,233	7,813	8,138
Malaysia and Singapore	0	372	262	1,355	2,495	6,485
Hong Kong, South Korea and Taiwan	0	48	23	66	1,762	917

Other	746	811	913	812	3,556	736
Latin America	2,201	5,047	6,202	4,580	2,866	5,898
Argentina	253	443	360	292	271	74
Brazil	56	455	874	745	53	1,942
Chile	187	256	336	159	335	344
Colombia	587	990	967	68	158	113
Mexico	448	1,193	1,408	1,757	851	736
Peru	398	384	413	679	469	624
Venezuela	123	1,045	1,358	221	267	278
Other	149	281	486	659	462	1,787
All regions	19,915	39,211	49,333	53,191	72,713	67,700

Table B.17. Total Swedish exports, by region, 1965–90. Current prices (MSEK)

	1965	1970	1974	1978	1986	1990
All developed countries	17,895	29,877	58,646	78,300	230,168	296,521
EC-6	6,384	9,694	18,164	26,239	76,394	112,309
EC-3	4,645	7,977	15,665	20,166	50,253	59,371
EC-south	616	879	2,415	2,149	6,015	12,202
EFTA	4,091	7,597	15,068	19,247	54,854	64,708
North America	1,473	2,594	4,748	7,430	33,908	34,160
Other developed countries	686	1,136	2,586	3,069	8,744	13,771
Eastern Europe	877	1,984	3,928	5,313	7,363	8,908
All developing countries	1,769	3,289	7,940	14,592	27,572	34,423
Africa	412	941	2,194	4,028	5,695	5,403
Asia	620	1,104	2,993	7,684	16,129	22,238
Latin America	737	1,244	2,753	2,880	5,748	6,782
All regions	20,541	35,150	70,514	98,205	265,103	339,852

NOTES

1 INTRODUCTION

1 In 1993, above 40 per cent of the world total was channelled toward the developing world (UNCTAD, 1994).
2 OECD, the Organization for Economic Cooperation and Development, consists essentially of the market-oriented industrialized economies.
3 A separate questionnaire has been collected for each manufacturing affiliate, covering employment, trade, financial statistics, etc. See further Appendix A.
4 Information on specific issues is available for more than 119 companies. In order to attain comparability between measures, however, the information reported is limited throughout the book to these corporations.
5 It should be noted that the information presented in Appendix B is based on the affiliate's industry in order to ensure comparability with previous work on the IUI database.
6 Reinvested profits are not reported by sector in central bank statistics.

2 MULTINATIONAL COMPANIES AND NATION STATES

1 See Lall and Streeten (1977) for further sources of oligopolistic advantage, the advantages of FDI with regard to trade, and the advantages of FDI relative to licensing.
2 UNCTAD (1993) refers to this as 'integrated international production'.
3 See also Swedenborg et al. (1988), Zejan (1989) and Andersson and Fredriksson (1994a).
4 See further OECD (1994b). ILO is the International Labour Organization.
5 Kokko (1992) reports evidence from the following countries: the United Kingdom, France, Germany, Canada, Australia, New Zealand, Mexico, Guatemala, Brazil and Malaysia. Japan appears to be the main exception, representing a case in which outward as well as inward FDI is rather associated with low concentration.
6 Externalities essentially represent costs or benefits which do not accrue to those who are responsible for them (Pigou, 1938).

3 SWEDEN AND THE INTERNATIONALIZATION PROCESS

1 Public expenditures correspond to almost 70 per cent of GDP, which is more than in any other economy. The average for the EC is below 50 per cent.
2 See, e.g., SOU (1993: 16), Andersson *et al.* (1993), NUTEK (1994), Eklund (1994), Henrekson *et al.* (1994) and Myhrman (1994).
3 Services have accounted for a growing share of export revenues, but the increase has been fairly marginal since the 1970s.
4 In July 1991, Sweden applied for membership of the EC. In January 1994 the European Economic Area (EEA) was formed, encompassing all EU and EFTA countries except for Switzerland and Liechtenstein. In a national referendum on 13 November 1994 a majority of voters supported Sweden becoming a member of the EU.
5 Again, the Swedish equity share of ABB, whose total number of employees exceeded 215,000 in 1990, does not exceed 50 per cent.
6 Whether to establish an affiliate in a certain country, and how much to produce in it, are interrelated decisions. This study includes both those countries in which MNCs have established operations and those where it has not done so.

4 MULTINATIONAL COMPANIES AND TRADE

1 In primary sectors, FDI mostly results in backward vertical integration, reinforcing trade in accordance with comparative advantage. In services, on the other hand, direct contact with consumers is normally required. Thus a local presence is often the only means of selling in a foreign market. Consequently, there is generally limited trade between affiliated units. Nevertheless, owing to the non-tradable character of many services, foreign sales tend to complement rather than substitute for exports.
2 The share fell notably in the late 1980s, partly as an effect of the merger between ASEA and Brown Boveri, which meant that ASEA was excluded from the population of Swedish MNCs. This partly explains the growing proportion accounted for by foreign-owned companies of Swedish exports.
3 In the UK, foreign-owned affiliates account for a greater part of exports, however.
4 By comparison, the export intensity of United States parent companies in manufacturing was only 12 per cent as of 1989 (UNCTAD, 1993). This, of course, mainly reflects the great difference in the size of the home market.
5 The growing importance of foreign affiliates as exporters has been noted also in the case of American and Japanese MNCs (cf. Encarnation, 1993; Blomström and Lipsey, 1990; Kume and Totsuka, 1991).
6 By 'intermediate' is meant here that a product is the output of one production process and input to another.

7 Moreover, a considerable amount of global intra-firm trade consists of imports by pure sales companies which merely resell what has been produced elsewhere.

8 A third category is capital goods, which account for a very small proportion of trade flows.

9 A similar observation was made for United States MNCs in Sleuwaegen (1985), who noted a high correlation between R&D intensity in the parent and intra-firm trade in both intermediate and finished goods.

10 Data on intra-firm exports to sales affiliates cannot be divided by country.

11 North American Free Trade Agreement.

12 These figures differ somewhat from those reported in Appendix A. In Table 25, affiliates have been grouped according to the industry classification of the parent company, while in the appendix the affiliate's industry has been used in order to enable comparisons to be drawn with earlier work on the IUI database.

13 See Pratten (1988) for a discussion of scale economies in the transport sector in the EC.

14 This will be further considered in Chapter 6.

15 The standard error for the group of greenfield ventures is as large as 1.33 for overall imports, 0.63 for imports of intermediates and 0.36 for imports of finished goods in 1974.

16 Foreign sales are here defined as total Swedish exports (including exports from domestic and foreign-owned firms in Sweden) plus net production by foreign manufacturing affiliates of Swedish MNCs (affiliate sales less imports from parents). A rising share means that total Swedish exports have grown more slowly than net production in foreign affiliates.

17 Analyses of data on industrial production confirm that Sweden lagged behind the trend in the OECD as a whole (Andersson et al., 1993).

18 A similar result is obtained when analysing the Swedish share of world exports of manufactured products.

19 If only countries which host manufacturing affiliates are included, the resulting estimates will be neither unbiased nor consistent. Compare, e.g., models which estimate how changes in real wages affect the labour supply. By excluding unemployed workers from the sample, a similar sample selection bias would arise.

20 The connection between affiliate and parent exports has not been thoroughly investigated previously. The issue is noted in Lipsey and Weiss (1984), but affiliate exports are never studied separately. The authors relate parent exports to a region to total and local sales respectively from affiliates in the same region, but not export sales explicitly. In addition, their model specification is somewhat arbitrary. Which measure of affiliate production is used for different industries is determined completely on the basis of the R^2-value in each regression.

5 TECHNOLOGY AND MULTINATIONALS

1 By way of a comparison, investment in fixed assets as a percentage of GDP fell in the early 1980s. R&D spending has consequently increased relative to physical investment.

2 If military R&D is excluded, the R&D intensity of the United States, France and the United Kingdom did not exceed 2 per cent in 1985.

3 Within certain guidelines, the definition of R&D was left to the companies themselves, 116 out of 119 MNCs answered the R&D questions in the 1990 survey.

4 This can be compared with an average growth of 2.6 per cent in GDP per annum in OECD countries during 1981–5.

5 An alternative measure of R&D intensity is R&D divided by value added. As in most studies concerned with the economic impact of R&D, we here apply turnover as a deflator (cf. Caves, 1982). Value added is generally more sensitive to economic cycles, but using it as a deflator would affect the patterns reported here only marginally.

6 Swedish R&D intensity equals Swedish R&D expenditure divided by turnover in the Swedish units. Foreign R&D intensity equals R&D expenditure in foreign affiliates divided by turnover in foreign affiliates.

7 Chemicals have the highest foreign R&D intensity of all industries. It amounted to 2.2 per cent in 1990, which can be compared with about 1.3 per cent for engineering.

8 Swedish R&D intensities for different industries are very similar to the total intensities shown in Table 34, although the latter are at a lower level. For further information, see Fors and Svensson (1994).

9 For individual MNCs in 1990, the Pearson correlation coefficients between the number of applications for patents, on the one hand, and R&D expenditure and R&D intensity on the other hand, were 0.73 and 0.55, respectively. Both are significant at the 1 per cent level. The number of observations equals 116. Similar patterns have been observed by Bound et al. (1984) and Pakes and Griliches (1984), who found very strong cross-sectional firm-level correlations between R&D expenditure and the number of received patents.

10 All foreigners accounted for 43 per cent of all applications in the United States.

11 See Mansfield et al. (1979), and Hirschey and Caves (1981).

12 There is some evidence that technology sourcing may serve as an important determinant of the localization of FDI in general, as in the case of acquisitions by Japanese firms in Europe and the United States (Anderson, 1993a; Yamawaki, 1994).

13 Foreign R&D amounted to SEK 4.6 billion in 1990 (Table 19). At least 65 per cent of this was undertaken in manufacturing affiliates. This figure is short of some missing values, however, meaning that the true share was even larger.

14 The Pearson correlation coefficient between the two variables amounts to 0.61, and is significant at the 1 per cent level.

15 As many as 35 MNCs had no R&D at all in foreign units, and 4 MNCs had 80 per cent or more of R&D abroad. In between, there are 44 firms with less than 50 per cent of R&D abroad, and 13 firms with at least 50 but less than 80 per cent located abroad. Finally, it can also be seen from Figure 12 that the 96 MNCs which did undertake R&D display a substantial dispersion around the weighted mean of 0.18.

16 See, e.g., Swedenborg (1979, 1982) in the case of Swedish firms, Lall (1980) and Kravis and Lipsey (1992) for United States firms, Hughes (1985) for British industry and Hirsch and Bijaoui (1985) using Israeli data.

17 Markets for technology are typically imperfect, accounting for high transaction costs for the sale of technology (Buckley and Casson, 1976; Teece, 1981). Thus the asymmetrical information and the cost of exercising control over the quality or diffusion of technology are commonly viewed as a major reason for internalization (Ethier, 1986; Horstmann and Markusen, 1987; Ethier and Markusen, 1991).

18 This relationship also holds when internationality is measured as a share of either exports from Sweden or foreign production. It becomes even stronger when the absolute values of R&D and foreign sales are related to each other.

19 See Katz (1969), Lall (1980), Blomström (1991), and Aitken and Harrison (1991).

20 The category of small manufacturing firms has between 20 and 200 employees, large firms have over 200, while subcontrators are defined by the dominance of a single customer. Subcontractors are of varying size, but have about 200 employees on average (Braunerhjelm, 1991).

21 For the population of Swedish MNCs as a whole there is a positive correlation of 0.28 between R&D intensity and training expenditure per employee, which is significant at the 1 per cent level.

6 EUROPEAN INTEGRATION AND RESTRUCTURING BY MULTINATIONALS

1 See Vickerman (1992) or Emerson (1988) for a comprehensive description of the Single Market programme.

2 With the Maastricht Treaty in 1992, the EC decided to deepen the economic integration and form an economic and political union (EU). In the late 1980s, however, these intentions were still unknown to investors and others and are therefore not considered here. The focus is on the plans for completing the internal market.

3 With regard to Austria, the insignificant movements have been attributed to the anticipation at an early stage that the country would eventually join the EC (Baldwin et al., 1994).

4 Austria applied for EC membership in June 1989, Sweden in July 1991, Finland in March, Switzerland in May and Norway in November 1992.

5 The somewhat higher figure for the EC in Table 47 is due to the exclusion of Turkey from the total.

6 Despite the noted increase in the number of Norwegian subsidiaries, employment fell by 25 per cent in Norway. Austria represents an exception among the EFTA countries with a positive growth exceeding 60 per cent.

7 The different picture in the latter country is mainly explained by the already mentioned acquisitions in the basic industry, as the companies that were taken over were highly export-oriented.

8 Truijens (1992) argues that France is an important exception in that local production by Japanese MNCs is there mainly motivated by difficult conditions for distribution and fear of discriminatory measures. As was reported for Swedish MNCs, this suggests a predominance of horizontal investments.

9 In order to attain comparability over time, the figures presented below concern only those for which information is available for 1986 as well as 1990.

10 The Expansion of intermediate exports applied to all sub-industries of engineering.

11 Value added is here defined as operating income before depreciation plus total expenditures on wages and salaries.

12 Cross-country comparisons of productivity levels are sensitive to currency fluctuations and measures undertaken by the MNCs with the purpose of affecting the intra-firm allocation of profits. Consequently, these observations should be interpreted cautiously.

APPENDIX A THE IUI SURVEY DATA

1 A similar investigation covering the years 1960–5 was carried out by Lund (1967). A mapping of employment in the foreign affiliates of Swedish MNCs was undertaken by Statistics Sweden in 1974 and co-ordinated with IUI for that year. For the late 1980s, close comparisons have been possible with the data of NUTEK (Swedish National Board for Industrial and Technical Development) and the Federation of Swedish Industries for the 20 largest Swedish firms in manufacturing.

2 In certain years, the questionnaire has also included foreign minority-owned affiliates (1965, 1970, 1974 and 1978).

3 Owing to these limitations, ASEA Brown Boveri is not regarded as a Swedish-owned company in the 1990 survey.

4 MNCs with exclusively foreign sales affiliates completed only the first part of Form A (questions 1–13).

REFERENCES

Aitken, B., and A. Harrison (1991), Are there Spill-overs from Foreign Direct Investment? Evidence from Panel Data for Venezuela, MIT and the World Bank, mimeo.

Åkerblom, M. (1993), Internationalization of R&D in Finnish Multinational Firms, Discussion Paper, Statistics Finland.

Aliber, R. Z. (1970), A Theory of Direct Foreign Investment, in Kindleberger, C. P. (ed.), *The International Corporation: A Symposium*, Chapter 1, MIT Press, Cambridge.

Andersson, T. (1991), *Foreign Direct Investment in Competing Host Countries*, Stockholm School of Economics, Stockholm.

Andersson, T. (1993a), Investment Asymmetry between Europe and Japan, Report No. 2, European Institute of Japanese Studies, Stockholm School of Economics, Stockholm.

Andersson, T. (1993b), Utlandsinvesteringar och Policyimplikationer, in Lindbeck *et al.* (1993), *Nya Villkor för Ekonomi och Politik*, Ekonomikommissionens Förslag, SOU 1993: 16, Bilagedel 1, pp. 85–107.

Andersson, T. (1994), Employment Effects of the Internationalization of Swedish Industry, Special Report for UNCTAD.

Andersson, T., and T. Fredriksson (1993), *Sveriges Val, EG och Direktinvesteringar*, Bilaga 7 till EG-konsekvensutredningen, SOU 1994: 6, Allmänna Förlaget, Stockholm.

Andersson, T., and T. Fredriksson (1994a), Distinction between Intermediate and Finished Products in Intra-firm Trade, Industrial Institute for Economic and Social Research (IUI), Stockholm, mimeo.

Andersson, T., and T. Fredriksson (1994b), International Organization of Production and Variation in the Exports from Affiliates, Industrial Institute for Economic and Social Research (IUI), Stockholm, mimeo.

Andersson, T., and R. Svensson (1995), Entry Modes for Direct Investment Determined by the Composition of Firm-specific Skills, *Scandinavian Journal of Economics*, 96, pp. 551–60.

Andersson, T., P. Braunerhjelm, B. Carlsson, G. Eliasson, S. Fölster, E. Kazamaki-Ottersten and K-R. Sjöholm (1993), *Den Långa Vägen*, Industrial Institute for Economic and Social Research (IUI), Stockholm.

179

REFERENCES

Baldwin, R. E. (1989), Growth Effects of 1992, *Economic Policy*, 9, pp. 247–82.

Baldwin, R. E., R. Forslid and J. Haaland (1994), Investment Creation and Investment Diversion: Simulation Analysis of the Single Market Programme, mimeo.

Becker, G. (1993), *Human Capital*, University of Chicago Press, Chicago.

Behrman, J., and H. Wallender (1976), *Transfer of Manufacturing Technology within Multinational Enterprises*, Ballinger, Cambridge, Mass.

Belderbos, R. A. (1992), Large Multinational Enterprises based in a Small Economy: Effects on Domestic Investment, *Weltwirtschaftliches Archiv*, band 128, Heft 3, pp. 543–57.

Bergsten, F., T. Horst and T. H. Moran (1978), *American Multinationals and American Interests*, Brookings Institution, Washington.

Blomström, M. (1991), Host Country Benefits of Foreign Investment, in D. McFetridge (ed.), *Foreign Investment, Technology and Economic Growth*, University of Calgary Press, Calgary.

Blomström, M., and A. Kokko (1994), Home Country Effects of Foreign Direct Investment: Evidence from Sweden, NBER Working Paper 4639.

Blomström, M., and R. E. Lipsey (1989), The Export Performance of US and Swedish Multinationals, *Review of Income and Wealth*, 35(3), pp. 245–64.

Blomström, M., and R. E. Lipsey (1990), Foreign Firms and Export Performance in Developing Countries: Lessons from the Debt Crises, NBER Working Paper 3412.

Blomström, M., R. E. Lipsey and K. Kulchycky (1988), US and Swedish Direct Investment and Exports, in R. Baldwin (ed.), *Trade Policy Issues and Empirical Analysis*, University of Chicago Press, Chicago.

Bound, J. *et al.* (1984), Who does R&D and who does Patents? in Z. Griliches (ed.), *R&D, Patents and Productivity*, University of Chicago Press, Chicago.

Brainard, S. L. (1992), A Simple Theory of Multinational Corporations and Trade with a Trade-off between Proximity and Concentration, MIT Sloan Working Paper 3492–92-EFA.

Brainard, S. L. (1994), An Empirical Assessment of the Proximity- Concentration Tradeoff between Multinational Sales and Trade, NBER Working Paper 4580.

Braunerhjelm, P. (1991), Svenska Underleverantörer och Småföretag i det Nya Europa, Forskningsrapport 38, Industrial Institute for Economic and Social Research (IUI), Stockholm.

Braunerhjelm, P. (1992), Industri-och Branschbegreppens Förändring, in *Sveriges Industri*, Industriförbundets Förlag, Stockholm.

Braunerhjelm, P., and B. Carlsson (1993), Entreprenörskap, Småföretag och Industriell Förnyelse 1968–91, *Ekonomisk Debatt*, 4, pp. 317–28.

Braunerhjelm, P., and R. Svensson (1994), Multinational Firms, Country Characteristics and the Pattern of Foreign Direct Investment, Industrial Institute for Economic and Social Research (IUI), Stockholm, mimeo.

Buckley, P. J., and M. C. Casson (1976), *The Future of the Multinational Enterprise*, Macmillan, London.

REFERENCES

Cantwell, J. (1989), *Technical Innovations in Multinational Corporations*, Basil Blackwell, Oxford.

Cantwell, J. (1990), A Survey of Theories of International Production, in C. N. Pitelis and R. Sugden (eds), *The Nature of the Transnational Firm*, Routledge, London.

Casson, M. C., and associates (1986), *Multinationals and World Trade: Vertical Integration and the Division of Labour in World Industries*, Allen & Unwin, London.

Cauvisqil, T. S. (1980), On the Internationalization Process of Firms, *Economic Research*, November, pp. 273–81.

Caves, R. E. (1971), International Corporations: The Industrial Economics of Foreign Investment, *Economica*, 38, pp. 1–27.

Caves, R. E. (1982), *Multinational Enterprise and Economic Analysis*, Cambridge University Press, Cambridge.

Cecchini, P. (1988), *The European Challenge 1992 – The Benefits of a Single Market*, Wildwood House, Aldershot.

Central Bank of Sweden (1992), unpublished data about direct investment in Sweden, Stockholm.

Central Bank of Sweden (1993), Foreign Direct Investment Statistics.

Cho, K. R. (1990), The Role of Product-specific factors in Intra-firm Trade of US Manufacturing Multinational Corporations, *Journal of International Business Studies*, 21, pp. 319–30.

Coase, R. H. (1937), The Nature of the Firm, *Economica*, 4, pp. 386–405.

Commission of the European Communities (1988), *Research on the Cost of Non-Europe*, Vol. 1.

Cooper, R., and A. John (1988), Co-ordinating Co-ordination Failures in Keynesian Models, *Quarterly Journal of Economics*, CIII, pp. 441–63.

Davidson, W. H., and D. G. McFetridge (1985), Key Characteristics in the Choice of International Technology Transfer, *Journal of International Business Studies*, 15, pp. 5–21.

Dunning, J. H. (1977), Trade, Location of Economic Activity and the MNE: A Search for an Eclectic Approach, in B. Ohlin, P. O. Hesselborn and P. M. Wijkman (eds), *The International Allocation of Economic Activity: Proceedings of a Nobel Symposium held at Stockholm*, Macmillan, London, pp. 395–418.

Dunning, J. H. (1981), Explaining the International Direct Investment Position of Countries: Towards a Dynamic and Developmental Approach, *Weltwirtschaftliches Archiv*, 117, pp. 30–64.

Eklund, K. (1994), *Hur Farligt är Budgetunderskottet?*, SNS Förlag, Stockholm.

Emerson, M. (1988), *The Economics of 1992*, Oxford University Press, Oxford.

Encarnation, D. J. (1993), *Rivals beyond Trade – America versus Japan in Global Competition*, Cornell University Press, Ithaca and London.

Ethier, W. (1986), The Multinational Firm, *Quarterly Journal of Economics*, 101, pp. 805–33.

Ethier, W., and H. Horn (1990), Managerial Control of International Firms and Patterns of Direct Investment, *Journal of International Economics*, 28, pp. 22–45.

REFERENCES

Ethier, W., and J. Markusen (1991), Multinational Firms, Technology Diffusion and Trade, NBER Working Paper 3825.

EC Commission (1994), *An Industrial Competitiveness Policy for the European Union*, Bulletin of the European Union, Supplement 3/94.

Feldstein, M. (1994), The Effects of Outbound Foreign Direct Investment on the Domestic Capital Stock, NBER Working Paper 4668.

Fors, G. (1993), Technology Transfer to Foreign Manufacturing Affiliates by Multinational Firms, Working Paper 370, Industrial Institute for Economic and Social Research (IUI), Stockholm.

Fors, G., and R. Svensson (1994), R&D in Swedish Multinational Corporations, Working Paper 370, Industrial Institute for Economic and Social Research (IUI), Stockholm.

Forsgren, M. (1989), *Managing the Internationalization Process: The Swedish Case*, Routledge, London.

Forsgren, M. (1990), Managing the International Multi-centre Firm: Case Studies from Sweden, *European Management Journal*, 8 (2), pp. 261–7.

Freeman, C. (1982), *The Economics of Industrial Innovation*, 2nd edition, Frances Pinter Publishers, London.

Geroski, P. (1988), Competition and Innovation, in Commission of the European Communities (CEC), *Research on the Cost of Non-Europe*, 2.

Graham, E. M. (1993), Transatlantic Investment by Multinational Firms: A Rivalistic Phenomenon, in J. H. Dunning (ed.), *The Theory of Transnational Corporations*, United Nations Library on Transnational Corporations, 1, Routledge, London and New York.

Griliches, Z. (1979), Issues in Assessing the Contribution of Research and Development to Productivity Growth, *Bell Journal of Economics*, 10, pp. 92–116.

Grosse, R. (1989), *Multinationals in Latin America*, Routledge, London.

Grossman, S., and O. D. Hart (1986), The Costs and Benefits of Ownership: A Theory of Lateral and Vertical Integration, *Journal of Political Economy*, 94, pp. 691–719.

Grubel, H. G. (1968), International Diversified Portfolios: Welfare Gains and Capital Flows, *American Economic Review*, 58, pp. 1299–314.

Guisinger, S., (1985), *Investment Incentives and Performance Requirements*, Praeger, New York.

Helleiner, G. K. (1979), Transnational Corporations and Trade Structure: The Role of Intra-firm Trade, in H. Giersch (ed.), *On the Economics of Intra-industry Trade: Symposium 1978*, J. C. B. Mohr, Tübingen.

Helleiner, G. K., and R. Lavergne (1980), Intra-firm Trade and Industrial Exports to the US, *Oxford Bulletin of Economics and Statistics*, 40 (3), pp. 297–311.

Helpman, E., and P. Krugman (1985), *Market Structure and Foreign Trade*, MIT Press, Cambridge, Mass.

Henrekson, M., L. Jonung and J. Stymne (1994), Economic Growth and the Swedish Model, Working Paper 19, Stockholm School of Economics, Stockholm.

Hirsch, S., and I. Bijaoui (1985), R&D Intensity and Export Performance: A Micro View, *Weltwirtschaftliches Archiv*, 121, pp. 238–51.

REFERENCES

Hirschey, M. (1981), R&D Intensity and Multinational Involvement, *Economic Letters*, 7, pp. 87–93.

Hirschey, M., and R. E. Caves (1981), Internationalization of Research and Transfer of Technology by Multinational Enterprises, *Oxford Bulletin of Economics and Statistics*, 42, pp. 115–30.

Horst, T. (1973), The simple Analytics of Multinational Firm Behaviour, in M. B. Conolly and A. K. Swoboda (eds), *International Trade and Money*, George Allen & Unwin, London.

Horstman, I., and J. Markusen (1987), Licensing *v.* Direct Investment: A Model of Internationalization by the MNE, *Canadian Journal of Economics*, 30, pp. 464–81.

Horstman, I., and J. Markusen (1992), Endogenous Market Structures in International Trade, *Journal of International Economics*, 32, pp. 109–29.

Hughes, K. S. (1985), Exports and Innovation: A Simultaneous Model, *European Economic Review*, 30, pp. 389–99.

Hymer, S. H. (1960), The International Operations of National Firms: A Study of Direct Foreign Investment, Ph.D. Dissertation, MIT.

International Monteary Fund (IMF), various issues, International Financial Statistics.

Japan Ministry of Finance (1991), *Kokusai Kinya Kyoku Nenpo*, Tokyo.

Johanson, J., and J-E. Vahlne (1977), The Internationalization Process of the Firm: A Model of Knowledge Development and Increasing Foreign Market Commitments, *Journal of International Business Studies*, 8, pp. 23–32.

Jordan, J. L., and J-E. Vahlne (1981), Domestic Employment Effects of Direct Investment Abroad by Two Swedish Multinationals, Working Paper 13, Multinational Enterprise Programme, ILO, Geneva.

Jungnickel, R. (1993), Foreign Direct Investment: Recent Trends in a Changing World, HWWA Report 115, Hamburg.

Katz, J. M. (1969), *Production Functions, Foreign Investment and Growth: A Study based on the Argentine Manufacturing Sector, 1946–1961*, Contributions to Economic Analysis 58, North-Holland, Amsterdam.

Katz, J. M. (1987), *Technology Creation in Latin American Manufacturing Industries*, St Martin's Press, New York.

Kindleberger, C. P., (1969), *American Business Abroad: Six Lectures on Direct Investment*, Yale University Press, New Haven.

Knickerbocker, F. T. (1973), *Oligopolistic Reaction and Multinational Enterprise*, Harvard University Press, Cambridge, Mass.

Kobrin, S. J. (1984), Expropriation as an Attempt to Control Foreign Firms in LDCs: Trends from 1960 to 1979, *International Studies Quarterly*, 28, pp. 329–48.

Kogut, B., and S. J. Chang (1991), Technological Capabilities and Japanese Foreign Direct Investment in the United States, *Review of Economics and Statistics*, 73, pp. 401–13.

Kojima, K. (1973), A Macroeconomic Approach to Foreign Direct Investment, *Hitotsubashi Journal of Economics*, 14, pp. 1–21.

Kokko, A. (1992), *Foreign Direct Investment, Host Country Characteristics and Spill-overs*, Stockholm School of Economics, Stockholm.

REFERENCES

Kravis, I. B., and R. E. Lipsey (1992), Sources of Competitiveness of the United States and its Multinational Firms, *Review of Economics and Statistics*, 74, pp. 193–201.

Krugman, P. R. (1980), Scale Economies, Product Differentiation and the Pattern of Trade, *American Economic Review*, 70, pp. 950–9.

Krugman, P. R. (1983), The 'New Theories' of International Trade and the Multinational Enterprise, in D. B. Audretsch and C. Kindleberger (eds), *The Multinational Corporation in the 1980s*, MIT Press, Cambridge, Mass.

Kume, G., and K. Totsuka (1991), Japanese Manufacturing Investment in the EC: Motivations and Locations, in Sumitomo Life Research Institute with Masaru Yoshitomi, *Japanese Direct Investment in Europe*, Billing & Sons, Avebury.

Lall, S. (1978), The Pattern of Intra-firm Exports by US Multinationals, *Oxford Bulletin of Economics and Statistics*, 40, 209–22.

Lall, S. (1980), Monopolistic Advantages and Foreign Investment by US Manufacturing Industry, *Oxford Economic Papers*, 32, pp. 102–22.

Lall, S., and P. Streeten (1977), *Foreign Investment, Transnationals and Developing Countries*, Macmillan, London.

Lindqvist, M. (1991), *Infant Multinationals – The Internationalization of Young, Technology-based Swedish Firms*, IIB, Stockholm School of Economics, Stockholm.

Lipsey, R. E. (1994), Outward Direct Investment and the US Economy, NBER Working Paper 4691.

Lipsey, R. E., and M. Y. Weiss (1981), Foreign Production and Exports in Manufacturing Industries, *Review of Economics and Statistics*, 63, pp. 488–94.

Lipsey, R. E., and M. Y. Weiss (1984), Foreign Production and Exports in Individual Firms, *Review of Economics and Statistics*, 66, pp. 304–8.

Loury, G. C. (1981), Intergenerational Transfers and the Distribution of Earnings, *Econometrica*, 49, pp. 843–67.

Lucas, R. E. (1990), Why doesn't Capital flow from Rich to Poor Countries? *American Economic Review*, Papers and Proceedings, 80 (2), pp. 92–96.

Lund, H. (1967), *Svenska Företags Investeringar i Utlandet*, Federation of Swedish Industries, Stockholm.

Mairesse, J., and M. Sassenou (1991), R&D and Productivity: A Survey of Econometric Studies at the Firm Level, NBER Working Paper 3666.

Mansfield, E., and A. Romeo (1980), Technology Transfers to Overseas Subsidiaries of US-based Firms, *Quarterly Journal of Economics*, December, pp. 737–50.

Mansfield, E. D., D. Teece, and A. Romeo (1979), Overseas Research and Development by US-based Firms, *Economica*, 46, pp. 187–96.

Markusen, J. R. (1984), Multinationals, Multi-plant Economies and the Gains from Trade, *Journal of International Economics*, 16, pp. 205–26.

Markusen, J. (1994), Incorporating the Multinational Enterprise into the Theory of International Trade, University of Colorado, Boulder, mimeo.

McFetridge, D. G. (1987), The Timing, Mode and Terms of Technology Transfer: Some Recent Findings, in A. E. Safarian and G. Y. Bértin (eds),

REFERENCES

Multinationals, Governments and International Technology Transfer, Croom Helm, London.

Michalet, C.-A., and M. Delapierre (1976), *The Multinationalization of French Firms*, Academy of International Business, Chicago.

Micossi, S., and G. Viesti (1991), Japanese Manufacturing Investment in Europe, in A. Winters and A. Venables (eds), *European Integration: Trade and Structure*, Cambridge University Press, New York.

Ministry of Finance (1993), *Utrikeshandel och Handelspolitik*, Bilaga 15 till Långtidsutredningen 1992, Allmänna Förlaget, Stockholm.

Minor, M. (1987), LDCs, MNCs and Changing Trends in Patterns of Expropriation, University of Tulsa, mimeo.

Myhrman, J. (1994), *Hur Sverige blev Rikt*, SNS Förlag, Stockholm.

Norgren, L. (1993), Industriföretags FoU i Sverige och Utomlands, FoU-relationer i Delar av Verkstadsindustrin 1970–90, NUTEK, Stockholm, mimeo.

NUTEK (1993), unpublished processed data from Statistics Sweden.

NUTEK (1994), *Näringslivets Tillväxtförutsättningar till 2010*, Bilaga 6 till Långtidsutredningen 1994, Ministry of Finance, Stockholm.

OECD (1989), *OECD Science and Technology Indicators 3, R&D, Production and Diffusion of Technology*, Paris.

OECD (1992), *International Direct Investment: Policies and Trends in the 1980s*, Paris.

OECD (1993a), *OECD Reviews of Foreign Direct Investment: Sweden*, Paris.

OECD (1993b), Main Economic Indicators 1993, 1.

OECD (1994a), *The Performance of Foreign Affiliates in OECD Countries*, Paris.

OECD (1994b), FDI and Employment, DAFFE/IME (93) 25/REVI.

Oxelheim, L. (ed.) (1993), *The Global Race for Foreign Direct Investment: Prospects for the Future*, Springer Verlag, Heidelberg.

Pakes, A., and Z. Griliches (1984), Patents and R&D at the Firm Level: A First Look, in Z. Griliches (ed.), *R&D, Patents and Productivity*, University of Chicago Press, Chicago.

Pearce, R. D. (1982), Overseas Production and Exporting Performance: An Empirical Note, University of Reading, Discussion Papers in International Investment and Business Studies 64.

Pigou, A. C. (1938), *The Economics of Welfare*, 4th edition, Macmillan, London.

Porter, M. E. (1991), From Competitive Advantage to Corporate Strategy, in *Michael E. Porter on Competition and Strategy*, Harvard Business Review Paperback 90079.

Pratten, C. (1988), A Survey of the Economies of Scale, in *Studies on the Economics of Integration*, Research on the 'Cost of Non-Europe' Basic Findings, 2, Office for Official Publications of the European Communities, Luxembourg.

Raff, H. (1992), Foreign Direct Investment versus Exporting when Product Quality is Unknown, Université Laval, mimeo.

Rauch, J. E. (1991), Productivity Gains from Geographic Concentration of Human Capital: Evidence from the Cities, NBER Working Paper 3905.

REFERENCES

Ravenscraft, D., and F. M. Scherer (1982), The Lag Structure of Returns to Research and Development, *Applied Economics*, 14, pp. 603–20.

Ronstadt, R. (1984), R&D Abroad by US Multinationals, in R. B. Stobaugh and L. T. Wells (eds), Technology Crossing Borders, Harvard Business School Press, Cambridge, Mass.

Samuelsson, H–F (1977), Utländska Direktinvesteringar i Sverige, Industrial Institute for Economic and Social Research (IUI), Stockholm.

Scaperlanda, A. E., and L. J. Mauer (1969), The Determinants of US Direct Investment in the EEC, *American Economic Review*, 59, pp. 558–68.

Schumpeter, J. A. (1939), *Business Cycles*, Vols. I and II, McGraw-Hill, New York.

Sleuwaegen, L. (1985), Monopolistic Advantages and the International Operations of Firms: Disaggregated Evidence from US-based Multinationals, *Journal of International Business Studies*, 16, pp. 125–33.

Smith, A., and A. Venables (1988), Completing the Internal Market in the European Community: Some Industry Simulations, *European Economic Review*, 32, pp. 1501–25.

SOU (1993), *Nya Villkor för Ekonomi och Politik – Ekonomikommissionens Förslag*, Allmänna Förlaget, Stockholm.

Statistics Sweden (1993), special print-out, Stockholm.

Statistics Sweden (various years), National Accounts.

Stevens, G. (1969), Fixed Investment Expenditures of Foreign Manufacturing Affiliates of US Firms: Theoretical Models and Empirical Evidence, *Yale Economic Essays*, 8, pp. 137–200.

Stubenitsky, R. (1970), *American Direct Investment in Netherlands Industry*, Rotterdam University Press, Rotterdam.

Svensson, R. (1993), *Production in Foreign Affiliates, Effects on Home Country Exports and Modes of Entry*, Industrial Institute for Economic and Social Research (IUI), Stockholm.

Svensson, R. (1994), Effects on Home Country Exports of Overseas Production, Industrial Institute for Economic and Social Research (IUI), Stockholm, mimeo.

Svensson, R., and G. Fors (1994), R&D and Foreign Sales: Evidence from Swedish Multinationals, Working Paper 423, Industrial Institute for Economic and Social Research (IUI), Stockholm.

Swedenborg, B. (1979), *The Multinational Operations of Swedish Firms*, Industrial Institute for Economic and Social Research (IUI), Stockholm.

Swedenborg, B. (1982), *Svenska Industri i Utlandet: En Analys av Drivkrafter och Effekter*, Industrial Institute for Economic and Social Research (IUI), Stockholm.

Swedenborg, B. (1991), Svenska Multinationella Företag och Produktiviteten, in P. Hansson, K. Krafft, L. Lundberg and B. Swedenborg, *Internationalisering och Produktivitet*, Expertrapport Nr 8 to Produktivitetsdelegationen, Allmänna Förlaget, Stockholm.

Swedenborg, B., G. Johansson-Grahn, and M. Kinnwall (1988), *Den Svenska Industrins Utlandsinvesteringar 1960–1986*, Industrial Institute for Economic and Social Research (IUI), Stockholm.

Swedish Patent and Registration Office (1994), special print-out, Stockholm.

REFERENCES

Sölvell, Ö., I. Zander, and M. E. Porter (1991), *Advantage Sweden*, Norstedts Förlag, Stockholm.

Teece, D. J. (1977), Technology Transfer by Multinational Firms: The resource Cost of Transferring Technological Know-how, *Economic Journal*, 87, pp. 242–61.

Teece, D. J. (1981), The Market for Know-how and Efficient International Transfer of Technology, *Annals of the American Academy of Political and Social Sciences*, 458, pp. 81–96.

Thomsen, S., and P. Nicolaides (1991), *The Evolution of Japanese Direct Investment in Europe – Death of a Transistor Salesman*, Harvester Wheatsheaf, New York.

Truijens, T. (1992), Japanese Manufacturing Investments in Europe, Report Presented at Danish Summer Research Institute, Gilleleje.

Tsurumi, Y. (1976), *The Japanese are Coming: A Multinational Spread of Japanese Firms*, Ballinger, Cambridge, Mass.

UNCTAD (1993), *World Investment Report: Transnational Corporations and Integrated International Production*, United Nations, New York.

UNCTAD (1994), *World Investment Report: Transnational Corporations, Employment and the Workplace*, United Nations, New York and Geneva.

UNCTC (1988), *Transnational Corporations in World Development: Trends and Prospects*, United Nations, New York.

United Nations (1991), *World Investment Report: The Triad in Foreign Direct Investment*, United Nations, New York.

United Nations (1992), *World Investment Report: Transnational Corporations as Engines of Growth*, United Nations, New York.

United Nations (1993a), *World Investment Directory: Developed Countries*, United Nations, New York.

United Nations (1993b), From the Common Market to EC 92: Regional Economic Integration in the European Community and Transnational Corporations, United Nations, New York.

United States Department of Commerce (various years), *Survey of Current Business*.

Venables, A. (1987), Trade and Trade Policy with Differentiated Products: A Chamberlinian-Ricardian Model, *Economic Journal*, 97, pp. 700–17.

Vernon, R. (1966), International Investment and International Trade in the Product Cycle, *Quarterly Journal of Economics*, 80, pp. 190–207.

Vernon, R. (1979), The Product Cycle Hypothesis in a New International Environment, *Oxford Bulletin of Economics and Statistics*, 41, pp. 255–67.

Vernon, R. (1983), Organizational and Institutional Responses to International Risk, in R. J. Herring (ed.), *Managing International Risk*, Cambridge University Press, Cambridge.

Vickerman, R. W. (1992), *The Single European Market*, Harvester Wheatsheaf, London.

Vickery, G. (1986), International Flows of Technology – Recent Trends and Developments, *STI Review*, 1, pp. 47–83.

Wernerfelt, B., and C. A. Montgomery (1988), Tobin's *q* and the importance of Focus in Firm Performance, *American-Economic Review*, 78, pp. 246–50.

REFERENCES

Wheeler, D., and A. Mody (1992), International Investment Location Decisions: The Case of US Firms, *Journal of International Economics*, 33, pp. 57–76.

White, R. E., and T. A. Poynter (1984), Strategies for Foreign-owned Subsidiaries in Canada, *Business Quarterly*, summer, 49(2), pp. 59–69.

Williamson, O. E. (1971), The Vertical Integration of Production: Market Failure Considerations, *American Economic Review*, 61, pp. 112–23.

Williamson, O. E. (1975), *Markets and Hierarchies, Analysis and Antitrust Implications, A Study in the Economics of Internal Organization*, Free Press, New York.

Williamson, O. E. (1979), Transaction Cost Economics: The Governance of Contractual Relations, *Journal of Law and Economics*, 22, pp. 233–61.

Yamawaki, H. (1991), Location Decisions of Japanese Multinational Firms in European Manufacturing Industries, in K. S. Hughes (ed.), *European Competitiveness*, Cambridge University Press, Cambridge.

Yamawaki, H. (1994), International Competitiveness and the Choice of Entry Mode: Japanese Multinationals in US and European Manufacturing Industries, Discussion Paper, Université Catholique de Louvain, Belgium.

Yoshihara, K. (1988), *The Rise of Ersatz Capital in South East Asia*, Oxford University Press, Oxford.

Zejan, M. C. (1989), Intra-firm Trade and Swedish Multinationals, *Weltwirtschaftliches Archiv*, 125, pp. 814–33.

Zejan, M. C. (1990), R&D Activities in Affiliates of Swedish Multinational Enterprises, *Scandinavian Journal of Economics*, 92, pp. 487–500.

INDEX

Printed in the United States
by Baker & Taylor Publisher Services